When the time was Right

Published by
The Bible Reading Fellowship
First Floor, Elsfield Hall
15–17 Elsfield Way, Oxford OX2 8FG
Website: www.brf.org.uk

ISBN-10: 1 84101 486 9
ISBN-13: 978 1 84101 486 9

First published 2006
10 9 8 7 6 5 4 3 2 1 0

Acknowledgments
Unless otherwise stated, scripture quotations are taken from the Holy Bible, New International Version, copyright © 1973, 1978, 1984 by International Bible Society, are used by permission of Hodder & Stoughton Limited. All rights reserved. 'NIV' is a registered trademark of International Bible Society. UK trademark number 1448790.

Scripture quotations taken from the Contemporary English Version of the Bible published by HarperCollins Publishers, are copyright ©) 1991, 1992, 1995 American Bible Society.

Scripture quotations taken from The Revised Standard Version of the Bible, copyright © 1946, 1952, 1971 by the Division of Christian Education of the National Council of Churches of Christ in the United States of America, are used by permission. All rights reserved.

Extracts from the Authorized Version of the Bible (The King James Bible), the rights in which are vested in the Crown, are reproduced by permission of the Crown's Patentee, Cambridge University Press.

Scripture quotations from *The Message*. Copyright © by Eugene H. Peterson 1993, 1994, 1995. Used by permission of NavPress Publishing Group.

Scripture quotations marked (NLT) are taken from the Holy Bible, New Living Translation, copyright © 1996. Used by permission of Tyndale House Publishers, Inc., Wheaton, Illinois 60189. All rights reserved.

Extracts from The Book of Common Prayer of 1662, the rights of which are vested in the Crown in perpetuity within the United Kingdom, are reproduced by permission of Cambridge University Press, Her Majesty's Printers.

Extract from 'The servant king' by Graham Kendrick © 1983 Thankyou Music.
Adm. by worshiptogether.com songs excl. UK & Europe, adm. by kingswaysongs.com
tym@kingsway.co.uk. Used by permission.

Extract from 'Thorns in the straw' by Graham Kendrick © 1994 Make Way Music.
www.grahamkendrick.co.uk. Used by permission.

A catalogue record for this book is available from the British Library

Printed in Singapore by Craft Print International Ltd

STEPHEN RAND

Bible readings for the Advent season

For Susan,
for Queenie,
for Carolyn and all at Kairos,
with thanks for so much encouragement and support.
And for Rosina Mary,
a first grandchild,
born as this book was coming to birth,
arriving on my birthday—just when the time was right!

'When the time was right,
God sent his Son,
and a woman gave birth to him.'

GALATIANS 4:4 (CEV)

CONTENTS

PREFACE

My wife Susan and I help to lead a small church in Wimbledon. We meet in the Odeon Cinema—cue my standard joke about belonging to the church with the most comfortable seats and the largest individual communion cup holders in the country. The church is called Kairos, and I readily confess that using a Greek word for the name jars slightly with the strapline that follows it: 'church for today'. One of our members discovered this in conversation with a Greek friend. 'Why is your church called Kairos?' he asked. Tim was on the ball: he had been listening in church. 'It's a Greek word meaning "now is the time",' he explained. 'In ancient Greek, perhaps,' said his friend; 'in modern Greek it means "weather".'

Just to add to the confusion, *kairos* is also used to mean 'time' in modern Greek, but it clearly does not have the same significance as of old. In ancient Greek it meant the proper moment, the crucial moment, the chance, the opportunity—emphases that have been built on by theologians so that the word has taken on almost a specific religious meaning. The coming of Christ is seen as the prime example of a *kairos* moment, a time in history when the pattern of events creates a crisis which is an opportunity but also demands a response. It was a *kairos* moment for the world two thousand years ago, and so it is for us each time Jesus comes to us by his Spirit. One of the aims of this book is to encourage every reader to experience the coming of Jesus once again—a real Christmas, a *kairos* Christmas.

The Bible tells us that Jesus was born when the time was right. It was not that God suddenly seized an opportune moment on a passing whim. It was the result of a plan, known before time itself, and more than two thousand years in execution, a plan in which individual human beings fulfilled their role in the delivery of God's plan. Advent is a reminder of God's plans and purposes: they are sure, they come about, and we all have a part to play. Jesus came at the right time, the time of God's choosing—but a time that was right because of people who, over centuries, had followed God's promptings.

This does not mean that these people became robots, incapable of making their own choices. God worked in and through their choices, made of their own free will, as they responded to their *kairos* moments of opportunity. Some were aware of the significance of their actions; many were not. In our Advent readings we will have the opportunity, in the context of tracing God's plans and activity in human history, to reflect on a number of the people linked to the story of Christmas. There are discoveries to be made: what it means to be in God's purposes, how we can be used by God, and how God works in the big sweep of human history and the minutiae of individual human lives as well. This Christmas, you can meet the kind of people God uses: the failures, the reluctant, the ordinary, the humble, the faithful and the persevering.

We all probably know the image of human history as a tapestry. We see it from the back: a mass of knots and stray threads, with no apparent pattern or design. But when it is turned round, we see it from the designer's perspective, full of life and colour, and forming a design full of clarity and meaning. A more elaborate version of the story tells of a master weaver directing an apprentice who is working from the back, unable to see the design. Should the apprentice make a mistake, the master weaver, being a great artist, simply works the mistake into the design. We can't always see the big picture, but God knows what he is doing.

This book is not a theological study of God at work in history; neither does it attempt to answer philosophical questions about predestination and free will. It is written from the perspective that the Bible is God's word and therefore tells the truth. As a history graduate who takes truth seriously, I am well aware of the challenges made to the historical accuracy of the Christmas story in particular. But this is not an academic history book; it is a book for those willing to spend a small time each day to be reminded once again of the truth of scripture and to reflect on its particular relevance to them in this Advent season.

Christmas was not, in itself, the plan. It was an enormously significant moment in what is still an unfolding picture. The purposes of God will be fulfilled by the ultimate and complete overthrow of evil and the release of the entire universe from the effects of sin—the completion of the victory won by Jesus when he died on the cross. And the greatest dimension of this plan from our perspective is that those who choose to put their faith and trust in the one who was born, who died and was raised from the dead, can play their part in the ongoing battle and share in the triumph of the victor—not as soldiers, not as servants, but as children, members of the royal family of heaven.

How great is the love the Father has lavished on us, that we should be called children of God! … Dear friends, now we are children of God, and what we will be has not yet been made known. But we know that when he appears, we shall be like him, for we shall see him as he is.
1 JOHN 3:1–2

Not long after Susan and I had become part of the leadership team at Kairos, we all met together one Sunday afternoon to pray and reflect on where we felt God was directing us as a church. We went to a retreat centre not far away, and, by one of those strange coincidences that we feel might be a little more significant than that, it too was called Kairos. In the entrance hall there was a little plaque, which said, 'Kairos—a Greek word meaning the favourable time or graced moment. This understanding of time is characterized by openness to the future. Now is the favourable time and Christ is its turning point. Kairos encourages us to be patient so we can let go and let God.'

May God use this book to encourage you and bless you through this time of Advent. May you let go and let God use you in his service as he fulfils his purposes in human history, in your history.

1–7 DECEMBER

THE FAMILY TREE

INTRODUCTION

Isn't it exciting when you know that someone wants to read the story of Jesus and explore it for themselves? You give them a New Testament, thrilled that they are going to sit down and give it a try. Then you remember: they will start at the first page, and they will get straight into that long list of names. That's if they get past the word 'genealogy' in the first sentence.

It is a salutary reminder that the Bible is an ancient book from the east rather than a modern book from the west. I knew when I started writing this book that I had to start with something interesting, to grab your attention. I'm hoping I achieved that: if you've got this far, I'm still ahead! But if I had started with a list of my ancestors...?

Genealogies are family trees, long lists of names that appear not only right at the beginning of Matthew's Gospel but also as a prelude to the ministry of Jesus in Luke 3. As a child, I was fascinated by the strange repetition of the word 'begat', one of the most colourfully archaic words in the King James Version. And even though they are the start of the Christmas story, these verses don't often feature in the average carol service: they are not ideal for public reading, packed with difficult-to-pronounce names that are largely unknown. But both Gospel writers used them to say something deeply profound about Jesus.

Luke works backwards. His family tree begins with Jesus (Luke 3:23) and, in 75 steps, takes his readers back to Adam, who is described with a great and certain finality as 'the son of God'. Matthew begins with Abraham, the father of the Jewish nation; Luke traces the line of Jesus back to the father of the human race. Matthew's Gospel is primarily written for Jewish readers, revealing Jesus as the promised Messiah; Luke is writing for Gentiles, and so he emphasizes the divine origin of common humanity.

Jesus did not arrive on planet earth as a space invader, an alien from beyond the stars. His advent was miraculous, certainly, but he was a human being with a family tree—antecedents.

My wife and I have just heard that we are to be grandparents! A new generation is to be added, a new line on the family tree. Of course, as we get older we tend to be more concerned to record our family history. We recognize that, as our parents advance in years, we risk losing their generational memory of half-forgotten great-aunts and deeply respected great-grandparents who exist for us in sepia tones on ancient photographs.

When my father died, we inherited our share of the family photographs. My wife was prompted to make several collages: one for ourselves that merged the Hicks/Hunt ancestry with the Rand/Kennedy line; one for each of our daughters that captured their childhood experience in the context of their relations. To us they are fascinating, an endless source of anecdote and memory; to visiting relatives they are an opportunity for exploration, of adding to the collective memory. And to friends, of course, they are no more than a curiosity, sometimes examined for signs of the origins of the peculiarities of the Rands that they find, we fondly hope, so endearing.

These collages inevitably spark one common topic of conversation: spotting the family likeness. The nose of this uncle, the eyes of a grandmother; it is a kind of biological jigsaw puzzle, always fascinating, never conclusive. Luke and Matthew were completely conclusive: Jesus was the son of Abraham, the son of David, the son of Adam, the son of God. It was from these antecedents that he gained his family likeness—his priestly royalty, fully human, fully divine.

Alongside that profound revelation, the family tree also indicates a paradox: the perfect man had a far from perfect family. There wasn't just one black sheep; there were several, almost a flock—the kind of people that it would be polite to gloss over. But Matthew and Luke are completely upfront. They know that part of the purpose of the family tree is to reveal that God's purposes are not worked out through saints but through sinners.

Here there is catastrophic failure, brokenness, rebellion, crime and treachery. There are women of ill repute, foreigners, high-born and low-born. In fact, as the newspaper advertisement used to say, 'All human life is here.' Exactly.

So let's begin Advent by turning a few pages of the family album.

1 December

ADAM: LET'S START AT THE VERY BEGINNING

God created human beings in his own image, in the image of God he created them; male and female he created them.
GENESIS 1:27

When the woman saw that the fruit of the tree was good for food and pleasing to the eye, and also desirable for gaining wisdom, she took some and ate it. She also gave some to her husband, who was with her, and he ate it. Then the eyes of both of them were opened, and they realized they were naked; so they sewed fig leaves together and made coverings for themselves.

Then the man and his wife heard the sound of the Lord God as he was walking in the garden in the cool of the day, and they hid from the Lord God among the trees of the garden. But the Lord God called to the man, 'Where are you?' He answered, 'I heard you in the garden, and I was afraid because I was naked; so I hid.' And he said, 'Who told you that you were naked? Have you eaten from the tree from which I commanded you not to eat?' The man said, 'The woman you put here with me—she gave me some fruit from the tree, and I ate it.'

Then the Lord God said to the woman, 'What is this you have done?' The woman said, 'The serpent deceived me, and I ate.' So the Lord God said to the serpent, 'Because you have done this, cursed are you above all the livestock and all the wild animals! You will crawl on your belly and you will eat dust all the days of your life. And I will put enmity between you and the woman, and between your offspring and hers; he will crush your head, and you will strike his heel.'

To the woman he said, 'I will greatly increase your pains in childbearing; with pain you will give birth to children. Your desire will be for your husband, and he will rule over you.'

To Adam he said, 'Because you listened to your wife and ate from the tree about which I commanded you, "You must not eat of it", cursed is the ground because of you; through painful toil you will eat of it all the days of your life. It will produce thorns and thistles for you, and you will eat the plants of the field. By the sweat of your brow you will eat your food until you return to the ground, since from it you were taken; for dust you are and to dust you will return.'

GENESIS 3:6–19

Have you ever tried to organize a traditional carol service? Fitting the readings together with the carols is always a challenge, and whichever edited version of the Christmas story you choose, someone will probably miss their favourite passage—and will probably let you know! When I worked at Tearfund, the annual carol service was always the last act of the year, with a staff choir giving up lunch hours for weeks beforehand to ensure a very high standard. Family, friends and former colleagues were invited, a guest speaker of repute secured, and members of staff delivered the readings with due solemnity and skill.

But the readings still had to be chosen. One colleague, an Anglican clergyman, insisted that, for the service to be complete, it was not enough to include Mary and Joseph, the birth at Bethlehem, the shepherds and the wise men. The first reading had to be from Genesis, the story of Adam and Eve. To him it was obvious: this was where the story of Christmas began. No rebellion in the garden of Eden? Then no baby in Bethlehem's manger. God opened the first window of his Advent calendar at the dawn of time.

Luke traces the family line back to Adam; when God speaks in the garden of Eden, there is the slightest hint that he is gazing down a line of history yet to be, looking forward towards Jesus. As the cataclysmic tragedy of the fall is recounted and its profound implications pronounced, hope is not quite extinguished.

I have vivid memories of reading *Voyage to Venus* by C.S. Lewis when I was a teenager. The hero travels to a planet untainted by sin, still in the beauty and innocence of the garden of Eden. Then he realizes that the history of earth is about to be played out again, as the inhabitants face the temptation of selfishness and rebellion. I cannot recall the details, but I do remember that I read avidly, desperately hoping against hope that the tragedy would not be repeated. Such was the strength of the writing that it was clear to me just how much hinged on the decision that would be made. Something beautiful beyond description would be lost, and the loss would be terrible, its ripples spreading out through time. Could that beauty ever be regained?

Genesis 3 reveals the awful catastrophe of sin, the devastating and all-enveloping impact of the fall. The forbidden fruit is eaten; the very first and immediate effect is that Adam and Eve are made aware of their nakedness, and cover themselves up. I used to feel very ambivalent about this passage in my youth: it seemed to offer such ammunition to those who were convinced that Christians were fundamentally flawed in their understanding of human sexuality—sin and shame, guilt and nakedness so closely bound together.

Now I see the passage as offering a profound insight into the reality of the human condition. At this moment of knowledge there is a decisive shift in the relationship between men and women. In the world that God created, they were equal inheritors and stewards of all that God had made, complementing each other in a mutuality of life and purpose. Now they are so aware of their differences that they have to cover themselves; from this moment, it is difference that dominates the relationships between men and women, mutuality and trust corrupted by exploitation and suspicion.

No sooner is their own relationship compromised than another terrible fracture is revealed. When God comes to walk with them, they hide in fear. Here is all the pathos and pain of a broken romance: the garden walk in the cool of the day will be no more. The human beings made in the image of God, for friendship and fellowship with him, are now hiding fearfully in the trees, pathetically imagining that they can go unnoticed.

Then they are turned out of the garden. Instead of caring for the creation they have damaged, they are faced with a battle for survival. Productive work becomes hard labour: 'cursed is the ground because of you; through painful toil you will eat of it'. Instead of participation in God's delegation of creative fruitfulness, there will now be suffering: 'with pain you will give birth to children'.

And death entered the reality of human experience: 'dust you are and to dust you will return'.

The devastation and despair were complete. The *shalom* of God—the peace that passes understanding, expressed in positive, life-giving and life-enhancing relationships for each human being with each other, with their creator God and with their environment—was shattered. The whole creation shares the agony: 'We know that all creation is still groaning and is in pain, like a woman about to give birth,' writes Paul (Romans 8:22, CEV).

But here is the hint of hope. To the serpent who had encouraged the disaster, God says that the woman's offspring 'will crush your head, and you will strike his heel' (v. 15). One reading of these enigmatic words is that there would be someone born in this family line who would one day pay the price and reverse the tragedy: re-creation, new life, reconciliation, *shalom* restored. 'For as in Adam all die, so in Christ all will be made alive' (1 Corinthians 15:22).

This is God's promise of intervention in human history, giving life to restore life. The Christmas story starts here. And it starts in the loving heart of Father God, creator of the universe, with Jesus—'the son of Adam, the son of God' (Luke 3:38).

Loving Father, creator of the universe,
fill our minds with wonder and thankfulness for all you have made;
fill our hearts with sorrow for all that sin has destroyed;
nourish our spirits with the hope that one day all will be restored.
Amen.

2 December

ABRAHAM: THE FATHER OF PROMISE

The Lord had said to Abram, 'Leave your country, your people and your father's household and go to the land I will show you. I will make you into a great nation and I will bless you; I will make your name great, and you will be a blessing. I will bless those who bless you, and whoever curses you I will curse; and all peoples on earth will be blessed through you.'

So Abram left, as the Lord had told him; and Lot went with him. Abram was seventy-five years old when he set out from Haran. He took his wife Sarai, his nephew Lot, all the possessions they had accumulated and the people they had acquired in Haran, and they set out for the land of Canaan, and they arrived there.

GENESIS 12:1–5

Advent is the ultimate reminder that God does not forget his promises. Thus, the hint of God's plan of new life and renewal found in Genesis 3 is given significant shape and content in these words to Abram, who will become Abraham.

It was, above all, a promise of blessing. What a lovely word! It has the overtones of all God's benefits being poured out with gracious generosity. It's full of positive content. Isn't it great when you call in on a friend, and as you leave they say, 'You've been a real blessing'?

In the definitive words of Aaron, there are such beautiful layers of meaning, all amplifications of what it means to be a blessing: 'The Lord bless you and keep you; the Lord make his face shine upon you and be gracious to you; the Lord turn his face toward you and give you peace' (Numbers 6:24–26). There are people whose presence represents these qualities; you feel encouraged and uplifted just to have spent time with them. Of course, their secret is that they have spent time with God: his Spirit has infused their spirit with God's own fragrance. We need more people like that.

God's message to Abram was also a promise of blessing for the whole world. Right from the start, God makes clear that he is not a tribal deity, tied in to one ethnic identity. He is the creator of the universe, God of the whole world, promising to bless—through Abraham—all peoples on earth. The inclusivity of the gospel is there from the start. Aren't you glad that God's kingdom encompasses every tribe and every nation? It means that there is a place for you! When, toward the end of the sixth century, Gregory the Great looked at a group of bedraggled, fair-haired English children being sold as slaves in Rome ('not Angles, but angels') and determined to ensure that Jesus was made known in that distant, damp outpost of the empire, he was recognizing that the good news is for every nation. In England we live in the inheritance that comes from his embracing of that fact.

This is one reason why racism in the church is such a denial of the gospel. How can Christians, citizens of the greatest multicultural kingdom of all time, so often descend to the fearful and ignorant prejudice that mistrusts, ignores, even abuses people of different ethnic groups? If God had behaved like that, we would have no Christmas to celebrate. It was because God loved the *world* so much that he sent his son (John 3:16).

My wife Susan and I were driving through Virginia on a Sunday morning, when we reached the town of Ordinary! We were rejoicing in this experience when it got better: we saw a sign to Ordinary Baptist Church! This was not to be missed. They were lovely people, and they gave us a warm welcome. In fact it was so warm that a young man, about 11, resplendent in a dark shiny suit, solemnly handed us a cardboard fan with a fading pretty picture and text on one side. As we lazily attempted to keep our cool, we discovered on the other side of the fan that it had been sponsored by the local undertaker: in the midst of life we were in death. The man leading the service asked if there were any visitors—and everyone swivelled round towards us. That was when we realized that we were the only white couple in the building. Later, I read that 11 o'clock on Sunday morning is the most segregated hour in the Southern states of the USA. It was, tragically, an ordinary Baptist church indeed.

God's blessing through Abraham was to be for all nations. God has always refused every attempt to be claimed by one culture. Of course, his inclusivity is the direct result of his exclusivity. If he is the one and only true God, then he has to be God for the whole world. It's wonderful when his followers embrace both realities in their worship.

If you had a plan to save the universe from destruction, where would you start? God's ways are not our ways. His promise was invested in the most unlikely individual. Abraham was not obvious material. He was getting on in years, and lived far from the right place. In one sense, it was as if God wanted to make absolutely clear that he was at work. He was the architect of his own promise. But let's remember that God chooses to work with and through flawed human beings to fulfil his purposes—flawed human beings who have to rise to the challenge and respond to God's calling. Abraham displayed some of the basic requirements for those who want to be used by God to be a blessing to others.

First, notice that Abraham heard God. From God's perspective, this is in character: he created the world by his word of power ('and God said...'). It was therefore perfectly logical that the great plan of salvation would begin with a word from God.

Perhaps it wasn't quite so straightforward for Abraham, though. From my own experience, I know that distinguishing the voice of God from a passing thought or even a good idea is both difficult and challenging: so much can depend upon it. I, at least, have the advantage of experience—my own and others'—to help my discernment. In a properly functioning church, there is a fellowship that can discern together when God has spoken.

Abraham had a lot less to go on, but the vital thing was that he was sure enough to take notice. He did what God said. It seems obvious, but I have met many who believe that the Bible is God's word and yet seem unwilling to take action on the things that it says. We sometimes long for God to speak and guide us, yet cheerfully ignore his written word.

Abraham was being asked to get up and move. That is exactly one of the questions that we often take to God for his guidance. I've spoken to dozens of people taking very seriously the possibility that God wanted them in another place, another country. It is a big question. I always emphasize that God is primarily interested in our willingness to serve him where we are and wherever we are, but I don't doubt the significance of the decision to leave behind all that is familiar because God asks it of us.

For Abraham, it meant leaving his people. Of course, the promise was that the willingness to obey would result in a new people, a great nation. That is always the pattern: when God speaks to move us on, he does so because he has something better in mind. But we must not minimize the challenge to Abraham. He was prepared to take risks on the basis of God's word. Now there's a principle for Christian living!

And, thank God, age was no barrier. These words mean a little more as I come to terms with becoming a grandfather. Please God, let me want to take risks for you as I get older. I know the truth: God still has a role for us in his kingdom, whatever our age. The question is whether I will believe it enough to seek it out and live it out. Abraham did, and became both the vehicle for God's purpose and a model for us all to follow.

The fulfilment of God's promise depends entirely on trusting God and his way, and then simply embracing him and what he does. God's promise arrives as pure gift. That's the only way everyone can be sure to get in on it, those who keep the religious traditions and *those who have never heard of them. For Abraham is father of us all. He is not our racial father—that's reading the story backwards. He is our* faith *father.*

We call Abraham 'father' not because he got God's attention by living like a saint, but because God made something out of Abraham when he was a nobody. Isn't that what we've always read in Scripture, God saying to Abraham, 'I set you up as father of many peoples'? Abraham was first named 'father' and then became *a father because he dared to trust God to do what only God could do: raise the dead to life, with a word make something out of nothing. When everything was hopeless, Abraham believed anyway, deciding to live not on the basis of what he saw he* couldn't *do but on what God said he* would *do. And so he was made father of a multitude of peoples. God himself said to him, 'You're going to have a big family, Abraham!'*

ROMANS 4:16–18 (*The Message*)

And because of what Jesus Christ has done, the blessing that was promised to Abraham was taken to the Gentiles. This happened so that by faith we would be given the promised Holy Spirit.

GALATIANS 3:14 (CEV)

Gracious Lord, grant me the courage to move when you call, and believe when you promise. Thank you for all the blessings I have received; help me to be a blessing to others. Amen.

3 December

ISAAC: THE LORD WILL PROVIDE

Some time later God tested Abraham. He said to him, 'Abraham!' 'Here I am,' he replied. Then God said, 'Take your son, your only son, Isaac, whom you love, and go to the region of Moriah. Sacrifice him there as a burnt offering on one of the mountains I will tell you about.' ...

Abraham took the wood for the burnt offering and placed it on his son Isaac, and he himself carried the fire and the knife. As the two of them went on together, Isaac spoke up and said to his father Abraham, 'Father?' 'Yes, my son?' Abraham replied. 'The fire and wood are here,' Isaac said, 'but where is the lamb for the burnt offering?' Abraham answered, 'God himself will provide the lamb for the burnt offering, my son.' ...

When they reached the place God had told him about, Abraham built an altar there and arranged the wood on it. He bound his son Isaac and laid him on the altar, on top of the wood. Then he reached out his hand and took the knife to slay his son. But the angel of the Lord called out to him from heaven, 'Abraham! Abraham!' 'Here I am,' he replied. 'Do not lay a hand on the boy,' he said. 'Do not do anything to him. Now I know that you fear God, because you have not withheld from me your son, your only son.'

Abraham looked up and there in a thicket he saw a ram caught by its horns. He went over and took the ram and sacrificed it as a burnt offering instead of his son. So Abraham called that place The Lord Will Provide...

The angel of the Lord called to Abraham from heaven a second time and said, 'I swear by myself, declares the Lord, that because you have done this and have not withheld your son, your only son, I will surely bless you and make your descendants as numerous as the stars in the sky and as the sand on the seashore. Your descendants will take possession of the cities of their enemies, and through your offspring all nations on earth will be blessed, because you have obeyed me.'

GENESIS 22:1–2, 6–18 (ABRIDGED)

Every time I read this passage, I find it shocking. Shocking because it presents us with a God who can demand child sacrifice and apparently be taken seriously. Shocking because it presents us with a man of God prepared to kill his only child because he has heard the voice of God. In our society, someone who prepares to kill their child having heard a voice is forced to receive psychiatric treatment.

So I am forced to begin with a historical perspective. Abraham lived in a world where child sacrifice was, if not common, certainly not unknown. Many people thought that devotion to their god could be tested by the demand to make this awful ultimate sacrifice. It may have been practised by some of the peoples of the land to which Abraham had been sent by God.

It is against this background that Abraham is developing his walk with God and his understanding of God. We have the Bible and the accumulated experience of two thousand years of Christianity to help us; Abraham had nothing to go on. He was forced to trust his own instincts, discerning the promptings of God and developing his understanding of what was expected of him.

It is in this context that the story begins not only to make some sense, but also to mark a significant step forward in human understanding of God. Isaac shared in the experience; it must have been terrifying, but it also anchored the new awareness of God's nature in the next generation. It means that we can even trace the route from the place called 'The Lord Will Provide' via a stable in Bethlehem to a cross outside Jerusalem.

The writer to the Hebrews saw this story as a story of faith. Abraham had faith great enough to believe that, if it became necessary, God could bring Isaac back to life in order to fulfil his promise (Hebrews 11:19). After all, God had already provided by performing a miracle to bring Isaac to birth in the first place. But his faith seems to have embraced an even deeper understanding of God.

His answer to Isaac, 'God himself will provide the lamb', is profound, even apart from the obvious echoes of the Easter story. Abraham's confidence in God was such that, even at this stage, he seemed to know that if he was prepared to commit all to God, then neither he nor Isaac could be the loser.

The Bible is full of references to the complete commitment that God expects of his people. Jesus even states it in terms of hyperbole that resonates with this story: 'If anyone comes to me and does not hate his father and mother, his wife and children, his brothers and sisters—yes, even his own life—he cannot be my disciple' (Luke 14:26). Few of us have experienced this kind of test. There are those in our world today who are forced to choose between their commitment to God and their family. What faith does it take to be forced to abandon wife and children because of conversion to Christ?

You may have been faced with a similar reality, even if not at this extreme. You may have sensed that God is demanding to come before someone or something very precious to you. I had a friend who knew that God was asking him to give up the potential of a professional music career in order to pursue God's best for his life. He discovered what Abraham discovered: that sometimes it is only when we are prepared to let go that God can really release his blessing. Within weeks, he had found a role using his musical gifts full-time within his service of God.

There's a sense, too, that God also showed faith in Abraham. He knew just how much Abraham loved Isaac. He also knew just how much Abraham loved God. The plan of salvation was safe.

So the promise is repeated and confirmed (vv. 17–18). At the point where Abraham has been prepared to end his family line, the promise is made specific that it will be through his offspring that all nations on the earth will be blessed. Here again is the mystery of God working in and through human history. Abraham knew that the initiative lay with God, and the miraculous method came from God: 'the Lord will provide'.

Isaac also learned on that traumatic day that human beings are included in God's plan. They are not pawns in a celestial game, but potential partners in blessing the world. His earthly father's faith was intrinsic to his heavenly Father's plan of blessing. Abraham was willing to obey a loving and trustworthy God, even at the moment when obedience seemed so shockingly unreasonable.

Isaac's life continued—a living symbol, twice over, of the truth that whatever the situation, whatever the test, the Lord will provide. The story of Advent is a revelation of the same truth: 'Look, the Lamb of God, who takes away the sin of the world!' (John 1:29).

God, who is rich in mercy and full of grace,
on the days when it is hard to trust you, build our faith;
on the days when all hope seems gone, remind us that
the Lord will provide. Amen.

4 December

JACOB: WHEELER AND DEALER

Jacob left Beersheba and set out for Haran. When he reached a certain place, he stopped for the night because the sun had set. Taking one of the stones there, he put it under his head and lay down to sleep. He had a dream in which he saw a stairway resting on the earth, with its top reaching to heaven, and the angels of God were ascending and descending on it. There above it stood the Lord, and he said: 'I am the Lord, the God of your father Abraham and the God of Isaac. I will give you and your descendants the land on which you are lying. Your descendants will be like the dust of the earth, and you will spread out to the west and to the east, to the north and to the south. All peoples on earth will be blessed through you and your offspring. I am with you and will watch over you wherever you go, and I will bring you back to this land. I will not leave you until I have done what I have promised you.'

When Jacob awoke from his sleep, he thought, 'Surely the Lord is in this place, and I was not aware of it.' He was afraid and said, 'How awesome is this place! This is none other than the house of God; this is the gate of heaven.' Early the next morning Jacob took the stone he had placed under his head and set it up as a pillar and poured oil on top of it. He called that place Bethel, though the city used to be called Luz.

Then Jacob made a vow, saying, 'If God will be with me and will watch over me on this journey I am taking and will give me food to eat and clothes to wear so that I return safely to my father's house, then the Lord will be my God and this stone that I have set up as a pillar will be God's house, and of all that you give me I will give you a tenth.'

GENESIS 28:10–22

What an opportunist! What a rogue! The Jacob we meet in this story does not seem to have inherited the faith of Abraham or the nobility of Isaac. He is out for himself, and his life seems to have been dedicated to overtaking his older twin brother. He was born holding on to his brother Esau's heel, as if already beginning the process of overhauling him to take the birthright and the blessing (Genesis 25:31; 27:36). The name Jacob means 'he grasps the heel', a phrase which was a figure of speech for deceit. What is not clear is whether it was Jacob's behaviour that created the figure of speech, or whether he simply lived up to his name.

This encounter with God takes place when Jacob is on the run and on a mission all at the same time. With his mother's connivance he has duped Isaac into giving him the blessing due to Esau as the firstborn. Esau has resolved to kill the deceitful Jacob, so mother Rebekah has a further cunning plan: Jacob can run to her family, and find a wife while he is there. Isaac is happy to command him to do just that. So Jacob is running from Beersheba, the family home, to escape Esau's fury and find a wife in Haran.

In these circumstances, it is amazing that he could put his head on a stone pillow and sleep at all, let alone meet with God in a dream! Perhaps the scheming had been exhausting; perhaps his conscience was not yet troubling him. But scientists tell us that we don't need long to dream—and it certainly doesn't take long to meet with God.

Jacob's dream had that familiar quality in which the images and realities of the waking world are woven into a parallel universe. Scholars seem certain that the stairway to heaven was a representation of a typical ancient ziggurat, a kind of pyramid with steps that enabled the worshippers to climb the sides until they came face to face with the deity who resided at the top. Jacob's dream reversed reality: the virtual ziggurat was a route to the true God.

This was the true God who confirmed and expanded on the blessing that Isaac had given Jacob—not the one gained by deceit, but rather the conscious handing on of the blessing to Abraham. Jacob discovered two things: that God himself was willing to affirm that even a deceitful rascal could receive God's blessing; and that this God was not just a local deity, but the God of the whole world, who could therefore watch over him wherever he went, however far he strayed from the family home.

Notice how Jacob reacts. It is as if this is the first time he has met with God for himself. This is the moment when he begins his personal learning, when the understanding handed down from his father and grandfather is brought to birth in his own experience. He had not realized that God was there; now he does. Mind you, experienced Christians can still be met with a new challenge, and flounder: it is amazing how easily new surroundings or new problems can leave us unsure of our confidence in God, and cause us to forget our past experience of his presence. Then we can be glad of the moment when we see signs of God at work, and say, with Jacob, 'Surely the Lord is in this place.'

I was brought up in a Christian home. I remain grateful for all I learned of God from my father and mother. I am even more grateful that, when I went to university and left home, I made my faith my own. We can gain knowledge, even understanding, from our parents and our upbringing, but we cannot inherit life-giving faith.

Jacob meets with God but he does not change overnight. He is a wheeler and dealer—and he is prepared to do a deal with God, on his terms. If God will deliver all that he needs, then he will make his commitment. Put as starkly as this, it seems incredibly immature, especially in the light of the blessing just given, unconditionally. Yet it is amazing how many people deal with God in this kind of way. Providing he delivers health, wealth and happiness, they will stay faithful. One friend of ours gave up on God because her mother was struck down with cancer, even though her mother's faith remained strong.

I have met many Christians in the poorest countries of the world who have nothing—no health and no wealth—but they find happiness in knowing God in the midst of their struggles. Material wealth always carries the danger of allowing us to buy our insurances, pay into our health plans and pension plans, and then look to God to fill in the gaps that we can't cover any other way. This was the danger faced by God and described by Moses, whose longing to see his people receive the blessing of the promised land was tempered by the realization that they would be tempted to rely on their wealth and forget the God who had provided it (Deuteronomy 8).

At Bethel, Jacob lays down his conditions to God—and when he returns from Haran he is ready to confirm his commitment. God gives him a new name, Israel. When he sets up a new altar, he names it for the God of Israel (Genesis 33:20). His father's God has become his God—but is it because God has kept his conditions? Later, in Bethel again, he builds another altar, for the God 'who has been with me wherever I have gone' (Genesis 35:3). This is the sovereign God who has kept his promise, not obligingly fulfilled Jacob's conditions.

Mighty God, who is from generation to generation,
thank you for every inheritance of faith we have received;
thank you for every scoundrel whose life you have turned around;
thank you for being with me wherever I go.
Amen.

5 December

RAHAB: TALES OF THE UNEXPECTED

Then Joshua son of Nun secretly sent two spies from Shittim. 'Go, look over the land,' he said, 'especially Jericho.' So they went and entered the house of a prostitute named Rahab and stayed there. The king of Jericho was told, 'Look! Some of the Israelites have come here tonight to spy out the land.' So the king of Jericho sent this message to Rahab: 'Bring out the men who came to you and entered your house, because they have come to spy out the whole land.'

But the woman had taken the two men and hidden them. She said, 'Yes, the men came to me, but I did not know where they had come from. At dusk, when it was time to close the city gate, the men left. I don't know which way they went. Go after them quickly. You may catch up with them.' (But she had taken them up to the roof and hidden them under the stalks of flax she had laid out on the roof.) So the men set out in pursuit of the spies on the road that leads to the fords of the Jordan, and as soon as the pursuers had gone out, the gate was shut.

Before the spies lay down for the night, she went up on the roof and said to them, 'I know that the Lord has given this land to you and that a great fear of you has fallen on us, so that all who live in this country are melting in fear because of you. We have heard how the Lord dried up the water of the Red Sea for you when you came out of Egypt, and what you did to Sihon and Og, the two kings of the Amorites east of the Jordan, whom you completely destroyed. When we heard of it, our hearts sank and everyone's courage failed because of you, for the Lord your God is God in heaven above and on the earth below. Now then, please swear to me by the Lord that you will show kindness to my family, because I have shown kindness to you.'

JOSHUA 2:1–12

Those who know me also know that I have a besetting sin: I am a terrible name dropper. In fact, I am so bad that I was just about to list some of the names that I drop; then I realized I would be found guilty again. My only defence is that I am constantly amazed that I, only too well aware of my ordinariness, have had the opportunity to meet people who are well known (some deservedly!). But I know that every time a name trips off my tongue, I have given in to the temptation to make myself look important by the company I keep (or, more accurately, people with whom I might have been in the same room for a few minutes).

Then there are the people we *don't* mention. Do you remember Hyacinth Bucket (pronounced 'Bouquet', of course) in the BBC sitcom *Keeping Up Appearances*? Much of the humour stemmed from her constant embarrassment at the appearance and behaviour of her sisters—so much so that she would often be tempted to disown them.

It has to be said that Rahab was not the most obvious person to mention in Jesus' family tree. She was a woman, a foreigner, a prostitute, a liar and a traitor: from various perspectives these would be good reasons to gloss over her place in the ancestry. But not only does her name appear in the genealogy in Matthew, she is also mentioned in Hebrews as one of the heroes/heroines of faith, and quoted as an example of doing the right thing by James.

It is just possible that Rahab was an innkeeper. This is a possible meaning of the Hebrew word translated 'prostitute', and it would offer an alternative explanation as to why the men went straight to her house. There is evidence from the ancient world, of course, that in many cultures innkeeping and prostitution were closely related. In some parts of the world, this would still be true. I remember meeting a young man in Uganda more than ten years ago. He had just been pronounced HIV positive, and he had determined to spend whatever months he had left, trying to ensure that others did not find themselves unwittingly infected with this deadly disease. He told me he had been a lorry driver's assistant, driving the long route through Uganda down to Kenya. Every night, when he went to his room in the town's local hostelry, a girl would be waiting, provided for him by his employer. It was part of the culture of the time—and the effects have been drastic.

Rahab is not particularly noble or spiritual in her motives. She has heard what God has done; she is convinced that Jericho is doomed; she wants to save herself and her family. It isn't much, but it is enough. She is prepared to risk her life to save her life. She has correctly identified the greater risk. So she hides the men, lies to protect them, and assists them in their mission. Her life is spared, and her actions are remembered down through history: 'By faith the prostitute Rahab, because she welcomed the spies, was not killed with those who were disobedient' (Hebrews 11:31).

In James 2:24–26, Rahab is held up as an example of making the right choices:

So you see, we are made right with God by what we do, not by faith alone. Rahab the prostitute is another example of this. She was made right with God by her actions—when she hid those messengers and sent them safely away by a different road. Just as the body is dead without a spirit, so also faith is dead without good deeds. (NLT)

Rahab believed God enough to act on her belief. In one simple moment she became an example of faith and of action: enough to save her life and give her a walk-on role not only in the story of the Israelites entering their promised land, but in the ancestry of Jesus. Action that stems from faith can save a life. That's not a bad epitaph, and not a bad principle to bear in mind as we seek to serve God. So often, we are obsessed with getting our doctrinal beliefs just right. The evidence of the Bible is that God cares more about what we do because of what we believe.

Rahab is also a wonderful example of the truth that God is never ashamed of anyone who has faith in him; no one is outside the possibility of being part of his plan. While you may not identify with Rahab in any specific way, I know that many people are convinced they are not good enough, not qualified enough, not important enough for God. So have the faith of Rahab: believe that you can be part of God's plans for his world, and that God will never be ashamed of you. In fact, he will write your name on the palms of his hands, for all the world to see (Isaiah 49:16). God is the one who specializes in making ordinary people special.

Thank you, loving Father, that your arms are open wide
for all who will run towards you.
Thank you, gracious Father, for accepting me.
Please let my faith be turned into action
for the glory of your name. Amen.

6 December

RUTH: OPTING IN

Now Elimelech, Naomi's husband, died, and she was left with her two sons. They married Moabite women, one named Orpah and the other Ruth. After they had lived there about ten years, both Mahlon and Kilion also died, and Naomi was left without her two sons and her husband. When she heard in Moab that the Lord had come to the aid of his people by providing food for them, Naomi and her daughters-in-law prepared to return home from there. With her two daughters-in-law she left the place where she had been living and set out on the road that would take them back to the land of Judah.

Then Naomi said to her two daughters-in-law, 'Go back, each of you, to your mother's home. May the Lord show kindness to you, as you have shown to your dead and to me. May the Lord grant that each of you will find rest in the home of another husband.' Then she kissed them and they wept aloud and said to her, 'We will go back with you to your people.'

But Naomi said, 'Return home, my daughters. Why would you come with me? Am I going to have any more sons, who could become your husbands? Return home, my daughters; I am too old to have another husband. Even if I thought there was still hope for me—even if I had a husband tonight and then gave birth to sons—would you wait until they grew up? Would you remain unmarried for them? No, my daughters. It is more bitter for me than for you, because the Lord's hand has gone out against me!'

At this they wept again. Then Orpah kissed her mother-in-law goodbye, but Ruth clung to her. 'Look,' said Naomi, 'your sister-in-law is going back to her people and her gods. Go back with her.' But Ruth replied, 'Don't urge me to leave you or to turn back from you. Where you go I will go, and where you stay I will stay. Your people will be my people and your God my God.

Where you die I will die, and there I will be buried. May the Lord deal with me, be it ever so severely, if anything but death separates you and me.'
RUTH 1:3–17

Poor widow marries lord of the manor and lives happily ever after: it could be a Mills and Boon paperback novel. But the story of Ruth is no rose-tinted romance; it is a beautiful account of relationships, timeless in its humanity. It is full of love, grief, faithfulness, hardship, kindness and hope. It is packed with revealing detail and rooted in historical and cultural reality—a reality far removed from our own, yet of startling relevance in the developing world even today. It is one of those biblical accounts that send affluent Westerners scurrying to commentaries for explanations, while villagers in Africa and Asia simply recognize the experience and the dilemmas as their own.

The first verse of the book opens up a desperate vista of modern reality. 'In the days when the judges ruled, there was a famine in the land, and a man from Bethlehem in Judah, together with his wife and two sons, went to live for a while in the country of Moab' (NIV). Food shortage creates displaced people, what some might call economic migrants. Moving in search of food is, and has been, a common pattern of life for millions of people—each one, of course, an individual.

I know exactly where and when I learned that truth: Ethiopia, 1984. The week after Michael Buerk's news broadcasts had alerted the world to the awful extent of famine in Ethiopia, I was visiting a food distribution centre funded by Tearfund in what is now Eritrea. We had travelled from the capital Asmara, past burned-out tanks and through checkpoints, to the small town of Decamhare, where in previous years a pastor had established an orphanage that had now become the base for a significant programme of famine relief.

We were in a large compound. The gates had just swung open to allow two camels laden with sacks of grain to enter: they could have walked straight off a Christmas card. There were a few hundred people gathered, waiting for food, and I was charged with gathering some information from them. So, with the help of an interpreter I discovered Tiekle's story. It was simple; it was stark. After three years of struggle in the face of drought, which had seen her and her husband sell all that they had in order to survive, they had woken one morning and decided that they would walk in opposite directions in the hope that one of them would find some food. Tiekle had picked up her baby and walked 250 miles in one week, living off leaves and berries along the way. Now she had found food, but she never expected to see her husband again. She was 20 years old.

In Britain, the TV news had been about the millions facing hunger. I had met one, an individual—one who had to make choices, hard choices, about survival. She would have understood Naomi and Elimelech looking round their home in Bethlehem, taking in the scarcity it revealed, and deciding to walk in search of food. Tiekle would have identified with Naomi: they were both women effectively made widows by famine.

There was a spiritual as well as an emotional battle for Naomi and Elimelech. Bethlehem means 'house of bread'. They were setting off for a land where they would depend for food on a people with whom the people of Israel had always had a difficult relationship. There was even a law that stated, 'You must never, as long as you live, try to help the Ammonites or the Moabites in any way' (Deuteronomy 23:6). I have read commentaries which suggest that Naomi and Elimelech were turning their backs on God's blessing by abandoning Bethlehem for the pagan Moab. Naomi's family's deaths are seen as evidence of their sin. I would love to read what a commentary would say that was written by someone who has actually experienced famine.

Naomi had made a decision to leave Bethlehem; now she makes the decision to return. Her daughters-in-law start out with her, but when faced with the reality of leaving home and culture, it is only Ruth who is prepared to leave it all, embrace a new life and follow a new God, out of love for her mother-in-law. Her protestation of commitment has the power to move us centuries later.

Ruth was opting in. Her decision had ramifications far beyond anything she could have seen or anticipated. The loyalty and friendship she extended to a widow, a self-confessed 'bitter' older woman, was to result in her appearance in the family line of Jesus. She was a foreigner, outside of the promises of God as far as the people of Israel were concerned, but she opted in out of love and became part of the story of God opting in to his world out of love. Ruth represents all those who discover that, when love prompts them to do the right thing, the consequences are in God's hands of gracious blessing.

Dear God,
this Christmas we want to do the right thing;
this Christmas we want to show our love to you,
and the people you have made.
Make us mindful of how we can extend your Christmas
grace to others, whether close or far away,
so they will have cause to bless your name.
Amen.

7 December

BOAZ: A PATTERN OF KINDNESS

Now Naomi had a relative on her husband's side, from the clan of Elimelech, a man of standing, whose name was Boaz. And Ruth the Moabitess said to Naomi, 'Let me go to the fields and pick up the leftover grain behind anyone in whose eyes I find favour.'

Naomi said to her, 'Go ahead, my daughter.' So she went out and began to glean in the fields behind the harvesters. As it turned out, she found herself working in a field belonging to Boaz, who was from the clan of Elimelech. Just then Boaz arrived from Bethlehem and greeted the harvesters, 'The Lord be with you!' 'The Lord bless you!' they called back. Boaz asked the foreman of his harvesters, 'Whose young woman is that?' The foreman replied, 'She is the Moabitess who came back from Moab with Naomi. She said, "Please let me glean and gather among the sheaves behind the harvesters." She went into the field and has worked steadily from morning till now, except for a short rest in the shelter.'

So Boaz said to Ruth, 'My daughter, listen to me. Don't go and glean in another field and don't go away from here. Stay here with my servant girls. Watch the field where the men are harvesting, and follow along after the girls. I have told the men not to touch you. And whenever you are thirsty, go and get a drink from the water jars the men have filled.' At this, she bowed down with her face to the ground. She exclaimed, 'Why have I found such favour in your eyes that you notice me—a foreigner?'

Boaz replied, 'I've been told all about what you have done for your mother-in-law since the death of your husband—how you left your father and mother and your homeland and came to live with a people you did not know before. May the Lord repay you for what you have done. May you be richly rewarded by the Lord, the God of Israel, under whose wings you have come to take refuge.'

RUTH 2:1–12

I was brought up in the Open Brethren tradition. There, I've come clean. Right now you may be nodding sagely, murmuring to yourself, 'I thought as much.' If I mention this in a church, of any denominational persuasion, there is invariably someone who sidles up to me and confesses that they too share this blessing/handicap (delete as you think appropriate). And if you have no idea what I'm talking about, don't worry—just start at the next paragraph.

So in my youth I was introduced to the concept of certain people and practices in the Old Testament being described as a 'type' of Christ. In essence, it meant that they offered a pattern or a principle that was fulfilled in Jesus. This is a potentially rewarding approach that helps us to understand aspects of the Old Testament and fills out our understanding of Jesus. It is also capable of being overdone and becoming a dead end of ever more arcane exploration.

Boaz was one of those characters readily described as being a 'type' of Christ. Certainly the Boaz described in the book of Ruth is not only characterized by many of the great virtues that we see in Jesus—kindness, gentleness, thoughtfulness—but there is also the whole episode described in Ruth 4 based on the idea of the 'kinsman-redeemer', in which Boaz buys back Naomi's land and is married to Ruth as a result. There are some problems about the exact parallels: Boaz himself is not the immediate kinsman-redeemer as such, for example. And if this is all too precious for you, perhaps you will relate to a different parallel: if Ruth fits your image of a romantic heroine, then Boaz has a very definite feel of the Mr Darcy about him—although he does not seem to appear dripping wet at any point in the story!

The story is rooted in the ancient law of Israel, and Boaz is seen applying that law, giving the legal requirements a human face. Since the law came from God, infused with his values and ultimately fulfilled in Christ, it is not surprising that Boaz reminds us of the one who was to follow in his family line.

Much of the law was about the land. It belonged to God, and people were its stewards, caring for it on God's behalf and using its produce in a way that recognized the one who had made that production possible. When it came to harvest time, the farmer was instructed to leave the edges of his field unharvested so that those without access to land—widows, orphans and foreigners—would be able to 'glean', to collect grain from the crop that remained.

Boaz applies the law with gracious generosity. He guarantees Ruth protection, ensures she has water to drink, and later adds his own gift to the grain she has collected for herself. Then he takes the law of the kinsman-redeemer very seriously, and Ruth emerges honoured, remarried and blessed. Through her, Naomi is also honoured and blessed. The book of Ruth ends with Naomi, no longer 'bitter', holding her grandchild and surrounded by the rejoicings of the women of Bethlehem. The grandchild is named Obed, and becomes the father of Jesse, the father of David.

So both Ruth and Boaz feature in the family line of Jesus. Ruth had opted in, but in her initial response to Boaz she shows that she was very much aware that she was a foreigner, an outsider. Boaz was equally aware of her qualities as well as her choice. Her behaviour mattered more than her birth, since it stemmed from her character rather than her nationality. She was indeed richly rewarded by the Lord, the God of Israel, under whose wings she had come to take refuge.

Boaz stands as a reminder that living in God's world God's way will always be marked by humanity and by graciousness, putting the welfare of others at the top of our list of priorities. What a tragedy that so many people view Christians as dry legalists, squeezing the life out of living! What a tragedy that so many Christians provide so many reasons to justify this view! Jesus challenged the Pharisees on exactly this point: 'Woe to you, teachers of the law and Pharisees, you hypocrites! You give a tenth of your spices—mint, dill and cummin. But you have neglected the more important matters of the law—justice, mercy and faithfulness' (Matthew 23:23).

Jesus came to fulfil the law, demonstrating through three years of ministry and through his death and resurrection just what God's way of living looks like, full of life and full of love. The Christmas story is no more a romantic novel than is the story of Ruth. Both, at heart, are about love that leads to doing the right thing. Ruth's baby, Naomi's grandchild, signified that. The baby in the manger signifies it as well.

Loving, living Lord Jesus,
help us so to reflect your character
that others can see something of you in us.
Help us to live to the full in the light of your values.
Amen.

8–14 DECEMBER

THE KINGLY LINE

INTRODUCTION

The family tree has already revealed the character of its creator. He is the one who encourages and rewards faith, who honours the social outcasts, who includes the outsiders, who gives a second chance to scoundrels, who affirms the significance of women. All are highlighted, all are woven into the tapestry of the ancestry of Jesus, and all have their counterparts in the ministry of Jesus, as the Son of God reflects and lives out the values of his Father.

The magi came looking for one born a king; Pilate named him king as he died. But a stable and a cross are hardly the setting for royalty, at least not in human estimation. Centuries before, Israel had demanded a king, and now they looked for a new king who would restore the kingdom. David was the king as superhero: the fearless youth, the faithful friend, the victor in battle, the unifier of the nation, the founder of empire. David was also the one who received God's promise: 'Your house and your kingdom will endure for ever before me; your throne will be established forever' (2 Samuel 7:16).

So it was more than nostalgia that made people yearn for a return to the good old days. When would God keep his promise? The royal line had started well. Solomon, full of wisdom, had built the temple that David had envisioned. Then, disintegration began, with Solomon's wives distracting him from his focus on God, and disaster quickly followed as the kingdom was first divided and eventually destroyed, its people taken into exile and the royal line almost extinguished.

As we trace the bumpy history of Israel's royal family, however, we can see that God's promise is never forgotten, neither by God nor by those who remained faithful. God's patience is sorely tested. Some kings lead the people in the right direction; others join the slide to worship false gods and wallow in evil. If the family tree up until David is a mixed bunch of characters, the kingly line from David to

Jesus is no better: a mixed bunch wearing crowns. Jesus' ancestry was royal, but not always regal; there was majesty and there was mess. But God still kept his promise. For those of us who more readily identify with the mess than the majesty, that's a real encouragement.

8 December

DAVID: THE BROKEN KING

It was now spring, the time when kings go to war. David sent out the whole Israelite army under the command of Joab and his officers. They destroyed the Ammonite army and surrounded the capital city of Rabbah, but David stayed in Jerusalem. Late one afternoon, David got up from a nap and was walking around on the flat roof of his palace. A beautiful young woman was down below in her courtyard, bathing as her religion required. David happened to see her, and he sent one of his servants to find out who she was. The servant came back and told David, 'Her name is Bathsheba. She is the daughter of Eliam, and she is the wife of Uriah the Hittite.' David sent some messengers to bring her to his palace. She came to him, and he slept with her. Then she returned home. But later, when she found out that she was going to have a baby, she sent someone to David with this message: 'I'm pregnant!'

2 SAMUEL 11:1–5 (CEV)

David gets a good press! His place in the history of Israel was assured. He was the poet and musician, writer of so many of the majestic hymns of worship that we find in the book of Psalms. He was the child prodigy who became a national hero by killing the giant Goliath. He was the faithful friend to Jonathan while running in fear of his life. He established the kingdom based in Jerusalem. People were proud to know him; to be in his kingly line was a high badge of honour. He was the king chosen because he was a man after God's own heart (1 Samuel 13:14, NIV).

But he certainly was not perfect. He wakes up after his siesta on a warm afternoon and one glance leads him desperately astray. Is he not the monarch of all he surveys? He succumbs to the grubby temptation of lust, reinforced by the corrupting temptation of power. He risks the integrity of his army to cover his tracks and then resorts to murder by decree. It is a story that highlights all the shameful distortion of masculinity brought about by sin—and, amazingly, it is a story recorded in the Bible.

Here there is no airbrushing of history. David seems not even to have attempted to use his power to preserve his reputation. One of the things I learned from my university studies is that the history we have tends to be written by the winners, and we have to view their accounts with a healthy scepticism as a result. Embarrassments and crimes can be swept under the carpet. Even today I read of the memoirs of a relatively recent British Foreign Secretary, which happen not to mention British complicity in an almost genocidal war while he was in office.

David's reaction to his guilt when confronted by the prophet Nathan is as profound as his crime. He recognizes that, ultimately, his crime was not only against Bathsheba and Uriah: 'I have sinned against the Lord' (2 Samuel 12:13). The depth of his remorse and repentance is revealed to us in a most powerful psalm born out of this experience.

Generous in love—God, give grace!
Huge in mercy—wipe out my bad record.
Scrub away my guilt,
soak out my sins in your laundry.
I know how bad I've been;
my sins are staring me down.
You're the One I've violated, and you've seen
it all, seen the full extent of my evil.
You have all the facts before you;
whatever you decide about me is fair.
I've been out of step with you for a long time,
in the wrong since before I was born.
What you're after is truth from the inside out.
Enter me, then; conceive a new, true life.

Soak me in your laundry and I'll come out clean,
scrub me and I'll have a snow-white life.
Tune me in to foot-tapping songs,
set these once-broken bones to dancing.
Don't look too close for blemishes,
give me a clean bill of health.
God, make a fresh start in me,
shape a Genesis week from the chaos of my life.
Don't throw me out with the trash,
or fail to breathe holiness in me.
Bring me back from grey exile,
put a fresh wind in my sails!

PSALM 51:1–12 (*THE MESSAGE*)

Here is a man who has faced the truth about himself before God. While there are many people who have a very low self-image, there are others, especially us men, who live with a fairly good opinion of ourselves. We are not perfect, certainly, but we are nice to know, we enjoy our own company; we can even think we are doing God a favour by expressing our interest in him. It is very easy, however, for this to be a façade that crumbles in the face of a healthy dose of reality. The Book of Common Prayer can help us out: 'we have done those things that we ought not to have done; and there is no health in us.'

It can be difficult to get this right. Those who need constantly to be reminded of God's love for them and acceptance of them will seize on the prayer of confession as further evidence of their unworthiness. And of course this is the point: there is nothing in us that makes us acceptable to God—but Jesus has made us acceptable. God does love us, even when we fail him. At the same time, it is only really possible to appreciate this grace of God when we realize just how unworthy we are. I recall many years ago when this realization hit me. I can't remember what triggered it, but I do recall the almost uncontrollable sobbing that seemed to last for minutes as I faced the reality of my guilt before God, and once again received his forgiveness.

David's guilt took him to the depths. He was convinced that his sin had cost him his son. It was a very different man who went back to Bathsheba, and a very different man who praised God for the safe delivery of a baby boy nine months later. The child was given the name Solomon, which may be a play on the Hebrew word for 'peace', *shalom*. Nathan brought him another name, as from God: Jedidiah, which means 'loved by the Lord'. Even after our most awful behaviour, there is the promise of forgiveness, the possibility of peace, the assurance of love.

When Matthew mentions David in the genealogy of Jesus, he is emphasizing that Jesus came from the true kingly line, drawing on all the authority and authenticity that this connection would bring. Is it surprising that he also mentions Bathsheba? Wouldn't this also highlight the human frailty of the great king? Perhaps Matthew wanted to emphasize very deliberately that Jesus was, and is, a descendant of a king who discovered true greatness by being broken and receiving forgiveness and restoration. Jesus, who came to make it possible for all to know God's grace, was born of a family that exemplified God's grace in its own experience. He was indeed, in the words of the hymn, 'great David's greater son'.

Holy God, full of purity and light,
expose the poverty of our own goodness
and the reality of our sinfulness.
Loving God, full of grace and mercy,
grant us forgiveness and restore our peace.
Where there is pride, bring humility;
where there is brokenness, release healing and renewal.
Through Jesus Christ our Lord.
Amen.

9 December

SOLOMON: A WEALTH OF WISDOM

Before the entire congregation of Israel, Solomon took a position before the Altar, spread his hands out before heaven, and prayed,

O God, God of Israel, there is no God like you in the skies above or on the earth below who unswervingly keeps covenant with his servants and relentlessly loves them as they sincerely live in obedience to your way. You kept your word to David my father, your personal word. You did exactly what you promised—every detail. The proof is before us today!

Keep it up, God, O God of Israel! Continue to keep the promises you made to David my father when you said, 'You'll always have a descendant to represent my rule on Israel's throne, on the condition that your sons are as careful to live obediently in my presence as you have.' O God of Israel, let this all happen; confirm and establish it!

Can it be that God will actually move into our neighbourhood? Why, the cosmos itself isn't large enough to give you breathing room, let alone this Temple I've built. Even so, I'm bold to ask: Pay attention to these my prayers, both intercessory and personal, O God, my God. Listen to my prayers, energetic and devout, that I'm setting before you right now. Keep your eyes open to this Temple night and day, this place of which you said, 'My Name will be honoured there', and listen to the prayers that I pray at this place. Listen from your home in heaven and when you hear, forgive.

1 KINGS 8:22–30 (*THE MESSAGE*)

Solomon, of course, is famous for his wisdom. The Bible records that he had a dream in which God offered him anything he would ask. What would you have asked for? Solomon's reply suggested that he already had a measure of wisdom: 'Give your servant a discerning heart to govern your people and to distinguish between right and wrong.' It was the right answer. God's reply was, 'Since you have asked for this and not for long life or wealth for yourself, nor have asked for the death of your enemies but for discernment in administering justice, I will do what you have asked. I will give you a wise and discerning heart, so that there will never have been anyone like you, nor will there ever be. Moreover, I will give you what you have not asked for—both riches and honour—so that in your lifetime you will have no equal among kings' (1 Kings 3:9, 11–13).

When the Queen of Sheba came to visit, she was overwhelmed, as Solomon displayed his wealth and answered all her hard questions. She praised God because she saw the evidence that God had kept his promise: 'Not even half was told me; in wisdom and wealth you have far exceeded the report I heard' (1 Kings 10:7). Yet somehow I find it harder to relate to Solomon than to David. David was a boy who played with stones and killed giants; David was a man who gave in to temptation and received forgiveness. Solomon, on the other hand, was a king who had wisdom, yes, but alongside his wisdom he had all the trappings of monarchy—great wealth (as well as 700 wives and 300 concubines).

Solomon was determined to carry out one task that was bequeathed to him by David: to build a temple in Jerusalem to honour God. It took him seven years, and finally there was a home—a suitable home in Solomon's eyes—for the ark of the covenant, the great chest holding the tablets of stone that Moses had brought down from the mountain hundreds of years earlier. And on the day that the ark was put in place, Solomon showed his wisdom in the prayer that he offered, featured in today's reading.

Solomon recognizes that one of God's great attributes is that he keeps his promises. He is a covenant-making and a covenant-keeping God. As we trace this fragile-seeming line from creation to Christmas, there is a thread that runs through it all: God keeps his promises and works out his purposes. There are some days when we have to hold on to this truth through the hurricane force of circumstances, but there are also days when we can celebrate it as Solomon did: God does exactly what he has promised—in every detail!

Then Solomon voices another truth, even a paradox, vital to everyone who ever goes near a church building. Whether you designed one, gave money to help build one, or simply go to one on a Sunday, always remember this: God is not contained in the building; he cannot be restricted to the building; he is not in the building more than he is outside the building. A thousand years after Solomon, Stephen emphasized this fact to his accusers: 'the Most High does not live in houses made by human hands' (Acts 7:48). Paul, too, looked at the wisest people in Athens, surrounded by temples, and said, 'The God who made the world and everything in it is the Lord of heaven and earth and does not live in temples built by hands' (Acts 17:24).

I used to belong to a church that called the part used for Sunday services the 'Sanctuary'. There were some who thought that drinking tea and coffee in the hall next door was an acceptable end to the service, but frowned upon tea and coffee brought into the 'Sanctuary'. Of course, we all have our own sensitivities about what constitutes appropriate behaviour in a church building, but what matters most is that we always focus on honouring God, and not the building.

There is a paradox here. God cannot be contained within the building, but he can be found within the building. I'm not sure which is worse: being so concerned about the building—the flowers, the music, the windows, the pews and so on—that it becomes an alternative to God and a hindrance to worship, or turning up to a service with no expectation that God will be present and longing to speak to his people. Of course, people meet with God in all sorts of places: on trains, boats and planes, by towering waterfalls and on windswept moors. Mother Teresa met with God in the children of the gutters in Calcutta. I have known the presence of God in lofty cathedrals and in dusty shanty towns.

But when people cite the truism that the church is people, not a building, they are offering a clue to the whole purpose of corporate worship. A church building is the place where God meets his people when they come together, acknowledging his presence. Our faith is and must be a community experience as well as an individual one. If we cut ourselves off from community, we cut ourselves off from a deeper experience of God. It's something to do with the whole being greater than the sum of its parts.

Then again, it is because God lives with each one of us as an individual that there is such blessing to be gained from meeting together. We have the opportunity and blessing of discovering something of God in each other. As Paul writes, 'Don't you know that you yourselves are God's temple and that God's Spirit lives in you?' (1 Corinthians 3:16). Solomon prayed his prayer before all the people in his great temple building. It's a great prayer for any building where we want to meet with God. It's a great prayer for each of us as we try to understand what it means to be God's temple.

There was one thing that Solomon desired above all else: that God's name would be honoured in his temple, and that his prayers would be heard. Now that's wisdom.

Almighty God,
when we come together in church to seek your face,
in your mercy meet with us;
when we seek your face in the quiet of our own space,
in your mercy meet with us.
Fill our church buildings with worship and with your glory;
fill our lives with worship and with your glory.
Thank you that you hear and listen to our prayers.
Amen.

10 December

REHOBOAM: DISASTER STRIKES

Three days later, Jeroboam and the others came back. Rehoboam ignored the advice of the older advisers. He spoke bluntly and told them exactly what his own advisers had suggested. He said: 'My father made you work hard, but I'll make you work even harder. He punished you with whips, but I'll use whips with pieces of sharp metal!'

When the people realized that Rehoboam would not listen to them, they shouted: 'We don't have to be loyal to David's family. We can do what we want. Come on, people of Israel, let's go home! Rehoboam can rule his own people.'

Adoniram was in charge of the work force, and Rehoboam sent him to talk to the people. But they stoned him to death. Then Rehoboam ran to his chariot and hurried back to Jerusalem. Everyone from Israel's northern tribes went home, leaving Rehoboam to rule only the people from Judah. And since that day, the people of Israel have been opposed to David's descendants in Judah. All this happened just as Ahijah the Lord's prophet from Shiloh had told Jeroboam.

2 CHRONICLES 10:12–19 (CEV)

Disaster! The kingdom founded on the bright hope of David and established on the magnificence of Solomon is torn in two, and centuries of decline, despair and exile follow. Today's reading describes a deeply significant moment, a turning-point in the history of God's people. But it did not come out of the blue. Even here there are clues to the long-term tensions and pressures that contributed to catastrophe.

In this tribal society, national unity had often been fragile. North and south were separated by a strip of land occupied by non-Israelite peoples, a physical separation that could all too easily become political separation. When the people first came to Samuel and asked for a king 'such as all the other nations have' (1 Samuel 8:5), they were looking for a leader who would establish and symbolize national unity, lead them in battle and guarantee their security—the very things that God had covenanted to provide for them himself. The problem was not so much the demand for a king, which had been anticipated by Moses (Deuteronomy 17:14–20), but the demand for one who would not be subject to God as their king.

This was exactly where Saul, their first king, had gone wrong. After a good start, he turned away from God, and the results were disastrous. In a dreadful battle with the Philistines, three of Saul's sons were killed, and Saul took his own life (1 Samuel 31:6). The immediate result was division along the old fault-lines: David was anointed king of Judah, and part of the rest of the kingdom that was not under Philistine control recognized Saul's son Ish-Bosheth as king. There followed a period of murder and bloodshed, which came to an end only when David agreed a treaty with the elders of Israel and was recognized as their king.

David united the people by the force of his personality and the effectiveness of his rule. He established a kingdom that stretched from the Red Sea to the River Euphrates, and captured Jerusalem to make it the new capital city. But Solomon's rule, beginning in wisdom and magnificence, increasingly undermined that unity by his ever-growing demands on the people for labour and taxation—and by the spiritual corruption that resulted when Solomon placated his wives by accommodating their gods.

There was therefore a long history of simmering tension when Solomon died, and Rehoboam was immediately faced with the task of establishing his own credentials to be king. Judah was naturally loyal to the royal line descended from David, but the northerners shouted, 'We don't have to be loyal to David's family!' The treaty agreed with David needed to be renewed, and that required Rehoboam to demonstrate wisdom and diplomacy, not least because the northern tribes had an alternative king in mind: Jeroboam.

Rehoboam took advice: a good start. He went first to those who had advised his father Solomon, and they demonstrated that they had perhaps learned a little of Solomon's wisdom: 'If today you will be a servant to these people and serve them and give them a favourable answer, they will always be your servants' (1 Kings 12:7). 'Servant leadership' is a fashionable expression, though its meaning is difficult to pin down in terms of specific behaviour. My observations of church and business over many years, however, force me to the conclusion that people are far more willing to follow leaders who are genuinely interested in them as people and who have a vision that goes beyond their own position and status.

Sadly, Rehoboam was more persuaded by the macho alternative. The newer advisers, his own peers, belonged to the 'iron fist' rather than the 'velvet glove' management school, believing that leadership works best by taking control, showing people who is boss. It was a fatal misjudgment. Rehoboam's lack of his father's wisdom was demonstrated further when he sent the head of forced labour to try to continue the negotiations. Adoniram was brutally murdered, and the division of the kingdom was confirmed. The great achievement of David had been squandered within a generation. The writer of the book of Kings is clear that Solomon's turning away from God would reap this harvest; and when the crunch came, Rehoboam looked to worldly advice and made the wrong choices, choices that reinforced his father's failings.

The writer of Chronicles decides to concentrate on David's line, the kings of Judah. They were the ones who inherited the promise to David: 'Your house and your kingdom shall endure forever before me; your throne shall be established forever' (2 Samuel 7:16). They were therefore those whose line would lead to the Messiah who would restore the kingdom. And, sure enough, Rehoboam's name appears in the family tree in Matthew.

It is easy to criticize leaders. I know, I've done it myself! In recent years I have spent a little time observing leaders. As part of my involvement with the Make Poverty History campaign, I was in Gleneagles in Scotland when the G8 summit, attended by the leaders of the world's richest countries, was hosted by Prime Minister Tony Blair. I stood with others in front of television screens, almost bemused by the news of the London suicide bomb attacks as the awful truth was revealed bit by bit. The Prime Minister rushed to London, and then returned to continue to fight for an agreement on action for Africa. As I watched him at the press conference 24 hours after the bombs had exploded, I was reminded of the biblical injunction to pray for leaders. Whatever your opinion of Tony Blair, few of us would have wished to be in his shoes at that time.

Prayer is part of our democratic responsibilities under God, just as much as voting in elections and raising our voice on behalf of the voiceless. Of course, our prayers will not absolve leaders of their responsibilities, but we must be careful not to abdicate ours, especially if we are ready to criticize. The story of Rehoboam reminds us that the decisions of leaders can have enormous consequences. That's why we should pray for them.

Great God, the source of all power,
who welcomes the humble,
we lift before you all those who exercise power:
in nations, in business, in councils, in churches.
May they look to you for wisdom and,
in all their responsibilities, demonstrate care for people.
Protect them from pride; give them strength for each day.
Through Jesus Christ our Lord. Amen.

11 December

JEHOSHAPHAT: JUSTICE AND WORSHIP

[The prophet Jehu said to King Jehoshaphat] 'There is, however, some good in you, for you have rid the land of the Asherah poles and have set your heart on seeking God.'

Jehoshaphat lived in Jerusalem, and he went out again among the people from Beersheba to the hill country of Ephraim and turned them back to the Lord, the God of their fathers. He appointed judges in the land, in each of the fortified cities of Judah. He told them, 'Consider carefully what you do, because you are not judging for human beings but for the Lord, who is with you whenever you give a verdict. Now let the fear of the Lord be upon you. Judge carefully, for with the Lord our God there is no injustice or partiality or bribery.'

In Jerusalem also, Jehoshaphat appointed some of the Levites, priests and heads of Israelite families to administer the law of the Lord and to settle disputes. And they lived in Jerusalem. He gave them these orders: You must serve faithfully and wholeheartedly in the fear of the Lord.

2 CHRONICLES 19:3–9

I was brought up on that wonderfully over-simplified comic history book, *1066 and All That*; I dread to think how it affected my career as a history teacher! Very helpfully, it offered a complex and profound moral judgment on each of the kings of England: some were good kings, some were bad kings. It was as simple as that.

Sometimes the Bible seems to deal in similar summaries of the reigns of the kings of Judah and the kings of Israel. Jehoshaphat is definitely towards the positive end of the spectrum. He was the fourth king of Judah; he reigned from 873 to 849BC, overlapping with Elijah's time as a prophet in Israel. His record of achievement was impressive: 'he did what was right in the eyes of the Lord' (1 Kings 22:43), although he did not completely end the worship of false gods.

We are told that he set his heart on seeking God—and the next thing we read, he is giving instructions to judges. Some scholars see the book of Proverbs as a book of guidance for royal civil servants: I do not think it a coincidence that, when Jehoshaphat sought God, he found himself sorting out the law courts. Jehoshaphat himself (his name means 'God has judged') knew that there was a link, because he saw the courts as both answerable to God for their decisions and reflecting the character of God in their decisions. The guarantee of justice for human beings was to have judges who knew that they were serving the Lord—and knew that the Lord they served had no place for injustice or partiality or bribery.

Yet I meet so many Christians who are nervous when people talk of justice. It is as if they have decided that justice should be left to dangerous left-wing radicals. They are much more comfortable with the idea of 'righteousness', though. There was a time when my local railway station featured a Bible text poster: 'Righteousness exalteth the nation,' it proclaimed, with the King James Version text printed in an ancient Gothic-style lettering, which either emphasized its long-term biblical authority or gave an impression of old-fashioned morality, depending on your perspective.

About the same time, I was visiting Lima, the capital of Peru, characterized then by sprawling shanty towns spreading across the grey sand dunes, with ramshackle houses fashioned out of a few bricks, bits of wood and corrugated iron. I spotted one house with what looked, at first glance, to be a political slogan daubed boldly in bright paint across its makeshift front door. Then my extremely rudimentary Spanish took in the phrase: *justicia exalta a la nación*. It was the same Bible verse as on the English station, given an altogether different feel, not only by its context, but by the choice of word. It was not a false translation: Spanish does not have two different words for justice and righteousness. It also matched the original Hebrew word, which encompasses the truth that God is concerned with what is right—right in the domestic sphere, in family and individual life; and right in the civic and national sphere as well.

The verse is Proverbs 14:34: just one phrase out of all that advice to civil servants, and one phrase that Jehoshaphat was keen to emphasize to his judges. For many years I have been speaking in churches, encouraging Christians to take seriously another verse in Proverbs: 'Speak up for those who cannot speak for themselves, for the rights of all who are destitute. Speak up and judge fairly; defend the rights of the poor and needy' (Proverbs 31:8–9). If God is concerned about justice, then his people must be concerned about justice.

That was why I regarded it as such a privilege to be part of the team responsible for the Make Poverty History campaign, because it was rooted in the belief that poor people and poor nations require justice, not charity. Of course it is right for us to be generous to aid agencies such as Tearfund, but we must also be ready to raise our voices, to be concerned about justice. Otherwise we not only sell short those who are poor, but we sell God short as well.

After appointing the judges, Jehoshaphat faced a new challenge.

Some men came and told Jehoshaphat, 'A vast army is coming against you…' Alarmed, Jehoshaphat resolved to enquire of the Lord, and he proclaimed a fast for all Judah. The people of Judah came together to seek help from the Lord…

[Jehoshaphat said] 'O Lord, God of our fathers, are you not the God who is in heaven? You rule over all the kingdoms of the nations. Power and might are in your hand, and no one can withstand you… We do not know what to do, but our eyes are upon you.'

Then the Spirit of the Lord came upon Jahaziel… He said: '… This is what the Lord says to you: "Do not be afraid or discouraged because of this vast army. For the battle is not yours, but God's…"'

Jehoshaphat appointed men to sing to the Lord and to praise him for the

splendour of his holiness as they went out at the head of the army, saying: 'Give thanks to the Lord, for his love endures forever.' As they began to sing and praise, the Lord set ambushes against the men of Ammon and Moab and Mount Seir who were invading Judah, and they were defeated.
2 CHRONICLES 20:2–4, 6, 12, 14–15, 21–22 (ABRIDGED)

This is the sort of passage that preachers love. It includes so many basic truths, so pithily expressed. However straightforward the statement, though, when we face those moments when it seems that a great army has come against us, it is so easy to take on the character of Corporal Jones in *Dad's Army*, revealing his panic by running around shouting, 'Don't panic! Don't panic!' It might be worth getting a piece of card and writing out in big clear letters, 'Do not be afraid or discouraged. For the battle is not yours, but God's.' Then fix it by the mirror that you look into each morning.

Jehoshaphat was 'alarmed', but he didn't panic. He began by giving time to focus on God: proclaiming a fast was a sign of dependence on God and a sign of just how seriously the people were taking their desire to hear from God. And they discovered that when you seek God he is ready to answer. As Jesus said centuries later, 'Ask and it will be given to you; seek and you will find' (Matthew 7:7). Having heard from God, Jehoshaphat acted upon what he had been told.

He fought his battle in a manner not suggested in the military textbooks, however. Putting the church choir or the worship band at the head of the army might seem to be a comment on the quality of their music! In fact, it was the key to success. I've talked to many people who have discovered that worship is the starting point in defeating their fears and winning their battles. The words of worship used in that ancient battle could be the ones you need to use right now: the men sang their thanks to God and reminded themselves of his love—or perhaps they were reminding the enemy.

This was not a magic spell. Worship is rooted in the reality of who God is and the objective reality of what he has done and is doing for us. The God who loves us is the God who wins battles. Perhaps that's why the angel choir sang a hymn of praise that first Christmas morning.

Great God of justice, you are worthy of our praise.
Give us voices to speak up for the voiceless.
Give us voices to sing your praise.
When we face great challenges,
give us songs of worship to sing.
When we campaign and when we worship,
win great battles, we pray, O Lord. Amen.

12 December

HEZEKIAH: NO ONE LIKE HIM

In the third year of Hoshea son of Elah king of Israel, Hezekiah son of Ahaz king of Judah began to reign. He was twenty-five years old when he became king, and he reigned in Jerusalem for twenty-nine years. His mother's name was Abijah daughter of Zechariah. He did what was right in the eyes of the Lord, just as his father David had done. He removed the high places, smashed the sacred stones and cut down the Asherah poles. He broke into pieces the bronze snake Moses had made, for up to that time the Israelites had been burning incense to it. (It was called Nehushtan.)

Hezekiah trusted in the Lord, the God of Israel. There was no one like him among all the kings of Judah, either before him or after him. He held fast to the Lord and did not cease to follow him; he kept the commands the Lord had given Moses. And the Lord was with him; he was successful in whatever he undertook. He rebelled against the king of Assyria and did not serve him. From watchtower to fortified city, he defeated the Philistines, as far as Gaza and its territory.

2 KINGS 18:1–8

More than one hundred years and ten kings of Judah have passed since the reign of Jehoshaphat. There have been evil and murder, battles and idolatry, with occasional moments of turning to God. The story of the nations, Judah and Israel, as described in the history books of Kings and Chronicles, is one of spiritual battles as much as physical battles. The writers know full well that success in the spiritual battles is the only thing that can release victory when the armies clash on the battlefield. Yet, decade after decade, the people and kings who have been called to the worship of the true God sometimes wholeheartedly pursue false gods, and sometimes simply accommodate their worship, failing to realize that both approaches court total disaster.

It is as if the people of God are living out on the pages of history the spiritual truth discovered and experienced by so many individuals: that the choices of total rebellion or half-hearted commitment are, from God's perspective, the same choice—a rejection of whole-hearted commitment. God's demands are total, and they are exclusive.

For thousands of years, rulers, even whole societies, have found this characteristic of the Christian God profoundly irritating. Megalomaniac despots might demand worship for themselves, but the more common pattern was for empires to achieve some kind of stability by assimilation. If a new nation was conquered, space was made for its gods: add them to the list; build another temple. It was religious toleration, and, if it was to work, it required all religions to be tolerant. But the Jews, and then the Christians, wouldn't play the game. They kept insisting that their God was the only true God—and, moreover, that he demanded exclusive rights to worship.

Once again we find ourselves in a society where the public statement of such exclusive claims for worship is seen as unacceptably out of step with a tolerant and multi-cultural society. This is a reality that demands careful thought and wise action from Christians. How can we demonstrate proper care and compassion for those of other faiths and none, and at the same time fulfil the mandate given by Jesus that disciples should go and make more disciples?

This is what I believe Paul is touching on when he writes of 'speaking the truth in love' (Ephesians 4:15). Many Christians seem to think that this is a special permit for ripping fellow Christians to pieces with supposedly helpful criticism; rather, it is about holding on to the truth of God but always expressing it and living it on the basis of genuine love for others. If you love someone, you are not concerned to manipulate their behaviour, to get them to sign up to your way of thinking by any means possible, and you don't refuse to pay any attention to their beliefs and understanding. If you love someone, however, you will also want them to discover the reality of relationship with the living God as you have done.

It is deeply tragic that the history of the church is marred by the activities of those who believed that it was right, even acceptable, to force people into God's kingdom by conquest or torture. It is deeply tragic that Christian mission has sometimes succumbed to the lust for power rather than the mandate of love. The challenge we face in the 21st century is to live for God and love for God so that, in our own willingness to commit ourselves fully to him, we reveal his love to the world. There must be no compromise in our confidence in Jesus as *the* way, *the* truth and *the* life, or in our willingness to communicate it—but we must communicate it in a way that demonstrates what kind of way, life and truth he is.

Hezekiah held fast to the Lord. Through his battles with external enemies and with severe illness, he looked to God. He was a man who prayed: his prayers are recorded in the Bible for us. He was a man who repented, and discovered the power of repentance to change situations. He was committed totally to God, and he knew that that meant he could not allow God's people to accommodate the high places and the sacred poles of false gods. What's more, he was not afraid to face up to the possibility that, even within the worship of God, there could be idolatry.

Hundreds of years earlier, as the people of God wandered in the desert and wondered when their deprivation would be over, they faced yet another trial. Poisonous snakes appeared and the people cried to God in repentance. Moses was instructed to put a bronze snake on a pole—and those who looked at it would live (Numbers 21:4–9). Of course, it was God who did the miracle, but the people, not unnaturally, regarded the bronze snake as something special. It eventually became an object of worship in and for itself; its veneration as an ancient relic lapsed fatally into idolatry. Its origin as a life-saving gift from God had not prevented it from becoming a sacred pole indistinguishable from those of false gods. So Hezekiah was not afraid to commit what our society would see as an act of cultural vandalism, and the ancient bronze snake was destroyed.

How easy is it for God's people to substitute a valuable gift from God for God himself? All too often I hear of churches being torn apart by arguments over the use of the King James Version of the Bible, the 1662 Book of Common Prayer, the pews... The test has to be whether things that God has used in the past have become more important to me than God himself. Have I become blinded to what God wants to do today because I am clinging to the ways God did it in the past?

One of the delightfully disturbing things about God is that he is constantly surprising us by the way he chooses to work. He is an unchanging God, but he is far readier to adapt his methods to changed circumstances than his followers often are. Even as I write, I know how easy it is to see this fault in others than in one's self. We have to be careful not to think that because our preferred method is tried and tested, it must be God's way. We have to be careful not to think that because our preferred method is new and innovative, it must be God's way! But I have to say that, in my judgment, the church of every denomination has too often erred on the side of fossilization than radical renewal. Even a book of Advent readings is very traditional, and if we read it out of convention or habit, we will have missed the point: the vital question is whether it alerts us to the presence of the living God.

Hezekiah rooted out those things that were substitutes for the living God in the worship of the people. God will accept no substitutes—not even his church or a particular ministry, no matter how valuable. The incarnation reminds us that God was totally committed to us and to his world. Jesus was born into human existence and human experience. He demands and longs for us to take up his offer, to be born again into his existence, so that we can live his life and he can live in us. In the words of the carol, 'Cast out our sin and enter in, be born in us today.' It really can be Christmas every day!

Dear God,
I want to put you first.
I want to have no other gods but you.
Show me if there are things in my life that need to be removed.
Show me if my habits and convictions need to be brought into line with your will.
Help me to change where I need to change,
and to hold fast where I need to hold fast.
For Jesus' sake. Amen.

13 December

JOSIAH: RULING BY THE BOOK

Then the king called together all the elders of Judah and Jerusalem. He went up to the temple of the Lord with the men of Judah, the people of Jerusalem, the priests and the prophets—all the people from the least to the greatest. He read in their hearing all the words of the Book of the Covenant, which had been found in the temple of the Lord. The king stood by the pillar and renewed the covenant in the presence of the Lord—to follow the Lord and keep his commands, regulations and decrees with all his heart and all his soul, thus confirming the words of the covenant written in this book. Then all the people pledged themselves to the covenant.
2 KINGS 23:1–3

The king gave this order to all the people: 'Celebrate the Passover to the Lord your God, as it is written in this Book of the Covenant.' Not since the days of the judges who led Israel, nor throughout the days of the kings of Israel and the kings of Judah, had any such Passover been observed. But in the eighteenth year of King Josiah, this Passover was celebrated to the Lord in Jerusalem. Furthermore, Josiah got rid of the mediums and spiritists, the household gods, the idols and all the other detestable things seen in Judah and Jerusalem. This he did to fulfil the requirements of the law written in the book that Hilkiah the priest had discovered in the temple of the Lord. Neither before nor after Josiah was there a king like him who turned to the Lord as he did—with all his heart and with all his soul and with all his strength, in accordance with all the Law of Moses.

Nevertheless, the Lord did not turn away from the heat of his fierce anger, which burned against Judah because of all that Manasseh had done to provoke him to anger. So the Lord said, 'I will remove Judah also from my presence as I removed Israel, and I will reject Jerusalem, the city I

chose, and this temple, about which I said, "There shall my Name be."'
2 KINGS 23:21–27

The high peak of Hezekiah's reign was followed by the desperate low of Manasseh, Josiah's grandfather. Then Josiah's father Amon was assassinated and Josiah became king at the age of eight, in 640BC. Judah was still part of the weakening Assyrian empire, and as Josiah grew up he began to assert his own authority on the nation. Not only was Assyrian religion pushed back, but he also turned his attention to all the other forms of pagan religion that had returned after Hezekiah's reign.

Josiah had been king for 18 years when he decided it was time to restore the temple, to make it fit once again for the worship of God. It was a process that had an unexpected outcome. Somewhere in the temple a book was found. It was taken to the king, and when he heard what it contained, he realized that action was needed. Scholars have debated what exactly the book was. Clearly it was all or part of the writings of Moses, clearly it was something that had been lost or overlooked for many years, and clearly it contained something that made Josiah decide to take immediate action. The general supposition is that it may have been the book of Deuteronomy, and it may have been the promises of chapter 28 that had such an impact.

Those promises were simple and stark: if you live in God's land God's way, the land will provide all you need and you will have security from your enemies; if you live in God's land your own way, you will forfeit its wealth, its security and even your hold on the land itself. It was this understanding that informed the writers of the history of the people in Kings and Chronicles; it was the principle that made sense of their history. Jeremiah began his prophecies during Josiah's reign, and he pronounced a judgment in this vein to Josiah's son: '"Does it make you a king to have more and more cedar? Did not your father have food and drink? He did what was right and just, so all went well with him. He defended the cause of the poor and needy, and so all went well. Is that not what it means to know me?" declares the Lord' (Jeremiah 22:15–16).

The book was read; Josiah responded. He realized the danger that the people faced. He called them together, they heard the word of God, and 'the people agreed to do everything written in the book' (2 Kings 23:3, CEV). That resulted in the people coming together again to celebrate the Passover; it resulted in Josiah taking further steps to purify the land from occult practices. The Passover celebrated God's activity in saving his people from slavery. The book had reminded them that slavery was their destination if they did not change their ways and renew their focus on God and his ways.

The preacher in me can't miss the simple and obvious application of this story. Having found God's word, they had to open it and read it. Having read it, they had to respond to it. It changed their behaviour in worship and it changed their behaviour in society. It directed them towards God and away from spiritism and mediums, the substitutes that so many people look to for guidance and wisdom in a complex world. And I can't resist pointing out that Josiah's encounter with the word of God may have been the prompt that led him to being known for defending the cause of the poor and needy.

Christians believe the Bible to be the word of God, yet surveys show that the Christian church in Britain is characterized by less and less actual reading of the Bible, corporately in church and privately by its members. My experience in leading the Alpha course over a number of years is that one of its crucial moments comes in the very first week. The subject is 'Who is Jesus?' but much of the content is basic information about the Bible. I have found people absolutely fascinated to discover the detail about how we know we have the original texts that were written; how the books in the Bible came to be selected and agreed by the early church. If we want to explore the truth about Jesus, we need to have confidence that the source material can be trusted. For centuries within Christendom, the authenticity and authority of the Bible were taken as read, if you will excuse the pun. Now we live in an age that is highly suspicious of those who claim to base their entire lives on an ancient book.

I am convinced that churches need to do much more to help their members become adept at using the Bible. The preacher may want to emphasize the need for us all to follow the example of Josiah's subjects and do everything written in the book; the teacher will realize that, if that is to happen effectively, we need increasing wisdom to know how we can distil the principles of the behaviour that God expects of us from a book written for a very different society so many centuries ago. The preacher tends to feel that all the hearer needs is the preacher's own understanding; the teacher knows that people remember what they discover for themselves rather better than what they are merely told.

I get frustrated when I hear preachers who refuse to acknowledge that there might be any understanding of a passage other than their own. It helps to create an unhealthy tendency for dogmatic certainties in areas where a little humility would be more appropriate and more honouring to the King and his kingdom. I need to be clear and careful here. I am not suggesting that the Bible does not have authority. It is the only source for understanding the truth about God. But we also need to recognize that this authority is not extended to my particular interpretation of difficult passages, or to specific applications to complex issues in life today. For example, I believe very strongly that the Bible has much to say that is relevant to the debate about scientific research using human embryos, but it is unhelpful to suggest that there is only one possible biblical view.

That is why it is important for church leaders to equip church members to know how to use the Bible for themselves. I was deeply challenged by meeting a Christian leader in Mexico City. Saul Cruz had, with his wife Pilar, established in a remarkable way a Christian urban transformation centre in a desperately needy slum community. When their commitment and love first encouraged individuals in the community to want to explore the meaning of the gospel, Saul had to decide how this should be done.

The people were illiterate. It would have been simple for Saul to read the Bible to them and explain to them what it meant, but he chose a very different option. He wanted them to respond and react to the word of God for themselves, not to receive his interpretation. So he began with the stories of Jesus. He encouraged the group to act them out and then reflect on what the different roles they played revealed to them about the truth contained in the story. In one sense, it was the same impulse that drove so many pioneer missionaries to do so much work to deliver the word of God in people's own language. It would be the route by which they could discover God for themselves. And occasionally you will meet people who have found God simply by reading the Bible. Doesn't that build your confidence in the book, and, more importantly, in the God who caused it to be written by the breathing of his Holy Spirit?

We need that confidence, because the Bible presents us with challenges that need to be faced. There's one in this passage. Josiah did what was right, but it was not enough to cause God to turn away from the heat of his fierce anger. Not only does this seem unfair; it seems to deny the very truth that scholars assume Josiah discovered in Deuteronomy 28. There is perhaps a clue, though, in the absence of certain words. Jeremiah was positive about Josiah as a king—but he is silent about the impact of the king's reforms. The leader had done what he could; but was it enough to reverse the deep-seated corruption of the people? The frightening suggestion is that the roots of evil can go so deep that its impact can be felt for generations. Modern history should teach us that. That's why our society needs a church that understands the Bible, knows how to apply it in society, and lives by it in the power of God's Spirit.

Holy Spirit of God, we are full of gratitude for the revelation of God
you breathed into the pages of the Bible.
We humbly recognize that we need your continuing inspiration
to read it, to understand it, and to live it in our world.
For Jesus' sake. Amen.

14 December

ZERUBBABEL: GOD'S SIGNET RING

On the twenty-first day of the next month, the Lord told Haggai the prophet to speak this message to Governor Zerubbabel, High Priest Joshua, and everyone else:

Does anyone remember how glorious this temple used to be? Now it looks like nothing. But cheer up! Because I, the Lord All-Powerful, will be here to help you with the work, just as I promised your ancestors when I brought them out of Egypt. Don't worry. My Spirit is here with you. Soon I will again shake the heavens and the earth, the sea and the dry land. I will shake the nations, and their treasures will be brought here. Then the brightness of my glory will fill this temple. All silver and gold belong to me, and I promise that this new temple will be more glorious than the first one. I will also bless this city with peace.

HAGGAI 2:1–9 (CEV)

The word of the Lord came to Haggai a second time on the twenty-fourth day of the month: 'Tell Zerubbabel governor of Judah that I will shake the heavens and the earth. I will overturn royal thrones and shatter the power of the foreign kingdoms. I will overthrow chariots and their drivers; horses and their riders will fall, each by the sword of a comrade. "On that day," declares the Lord Almighty, "I will take you, my servant Zerubbabel son of Shealtiel," declares the Lord, "and I will make you like my signet ring, for I have chosen you," declares the Lord Almighty.'

HAGGAI 2:20–23

The clock of history has ticked forward another hundred years. The disaster of exile, feared by Josiah and predicted by the prophets, had come to pass. It had already been experienced by the northern kingdom at the hands of Assyria in 722BC; for Judah, the collapse quickly followed the death of Josiah. Nebuchadnezzar of Babylon conquered Jerusalem in 597BC and, eleven years later, destroyed it by fire after Zedekiah's rebellion, taking the people hundreds of miles away to the east.

The exile was deeply traumatic, not least because of the challenge to the authority of God as a result of the downfall of his people, and to the worship of God as a result of the destruction of the temple. Psalm 137:1–4 gives us some idea of the despair felt by the people:

By the rivers of Babylon we sat and wept when we remembered Zion. There on the poplars we hung our harps, for there our captors asked us for songs, our tormentors demanded songs of joy; they said, "Sing us one of the songs of Zion!" How can we sing the songs of the Lord while in a foreign land?

Yet some people looked for the hope of restoration, as prophesied by Jeremiah—and it came from an unlikely source. Cyrus the king of Persia captured Babylon in 539BC and immediately instituted a new policy: instead of carrying off the gods and religious artefacts of the vanquished peoples, as the Assyrians and Babylonians had done, he decreed that his subject peoples should be allowed to worship their gods once again. The Jewish exiles were permitted and encouraged to return to Jerusalem and rebuild the temple. Zerubbabel was a grandson of King Jehoiachin, the last-but-one king of Judah, who had been taken to Babylon along with 10,000 of his subjects. Now, 70 years later, Zerubbabel was one of the leaders of those who returned to begin work on the foundations of the temple.

They began in 536BC, but, after a few years, opposition forced a halt to the work. Then, on 29 August 520BC, two years after Darius had become king of Persia, God gave the prophet Haggai a word for Zerubbabel: it was time to get on with the work. The word of God came with a challenge over their priorities; it also came with an encouragement: 'I'm living and breathing among you right now. Don't be timid. Don't hold back' (Haggai 2:5, *THE MESSAGE*). The encouragement was reinforced with a reminder of God's power and authority. The very things that the exile had seemed to undermine were to be demonstrated in a dramatic new start: 'I am about to shake up everything, to turn everything upside down and start over from top to bottom—overthrow governments, destroy foreign powers, dismantle the world of weapons and armaments, throw armies into confusion' (Haggai 2:21–22, *The Message*).

God's words through his prophet reinforce the message of the historians of Kings and Chronicles. The exile was not the result of God's failure but of the people's failure; because he was a God of love, however, and a God who kept his promises, there would be renewal and restoration. His power would be seen—not just in the turmoil of the nations, but in the life of one of his faithful followers. Zerubbabel had been chosen to perform this great task, and he was to be like God's signet ring, carrying the sign of God's sovereign presence and authority. The signet ring was pressed down into the wax seal on official proclamations, giving them the authority of the king: that was to be the role of Zerubbabel as the work of rebuilding the temple was restarted and completed.

Some people love to be chosen. Sometimes I stand at the front of a church, about to deliver a children's talk, and I ask for volunteers. Some children will almost burst in their desire to raise their arms, half-climb out of their seats and make themselves look as large and enthusiastic as possible in the hope that they will be the one. But not everyone is like that. Some are terrified of being picked out. They are the ones who would like to shrink into nothing when the person at the front is casting their eyes round, looking for volunteers. Some close their eyes, on the basis that if they can't see the chooser, then the chooser can't possibly see them.

So whenever I talk about God choosing people, I try to remember that people will react very differently to this concept. Some will revel and rejoice in it. At best, it will energize them and encourage them to use their gifts and skills in the service of God. At worst, it will confirm their high opinion of themselves and risk boosting their pride and levels of comfort and relaxation to unacceptable levels.

These are the people who need to be reminded that God's choosing is an act of grace to the unworthy, not a reward for services rendered. In fact, it is a commission to become part of God's plan and purpose.

Others find it hard to believe that they could ever be wanted by God. I have met Christians who can never grasp that God actually wants their company because he values them as individuals. They can be very nervous of being chosen, because their lives have been shaped by real or imagined failures—by teachers or parents who told them they would never amount to anything. To them, being chosen can simply mean being set up for failure and humiliation. These are the people who need to be reminded of God's love, that his Father's heart is as the heart of a father should be, and that he has promised that those he chooses will also be equipped by the gift of his Spirit.

Whichever category you may be in, there is one vital common factor: everyone who is chosen is chosen not just to have their name on the team sheet, but to play a vital role. There is a job to be done, and each has a unique input. Zerubbabel had his role in the rebuilding of the temple, authorized by God. He had a role too in the skein of history that led to the coming of Jesus. We have been chosen to be the children of God, and we have a part to play in a big picture that we can scarcely comprehend, but the final reel will feature the second coming of Jesus. Meanwhile, our lives have purpose. What could be more encouraging than that? Don't be timid. Don't hold back.

God, there are things I don't understand,
but I confess I am grateful that you want my company
and that you have things for me to do in your service.
As you reach out your hand to me,
give me the confidence to reach out to you and grasp your hand
so that we may walk—and work—together. Amen.

15–21 DECEMBER

A CAST OF THOUSANDS

INTRODUCTION

Some of them appear in the nativity plays; some of them don't. Every historical event has a list of *dramatis personae*. Some are the key players, with significant speaking roles; some have minor roles, but none the less significant. Then there are the extras, usually not named, but without whom the great events of history would become kitchen-sink dramas—entertaining, but with no wider or lasting significance other than for the protagonists.

Susan and I are among those who remain in the cinema to watch the titles roll up the screen when the film has ended. There are probably two reasons, apart from simply making sure we get full value for our ticket money. The first is that occasionally there are out-takes from the film worked into the credits: they are entertaining, and we feel so smug when we can say that we saw them, when those who made rapidly for the exits have missed them. The second is that we have a friend who works on films from time to time as an accountant, and whose name we have seen coming up on the screen, admittedly about four minutes after the cinema has otherwise emptied. But one fact always stands out from those credit sequences: doesn't it take an enormous number of people to make a film?

It certainly takes an enormous number to make history, including those who record it so that we know it *is* history. That tells me two things. The first is that the outworking of God's purpose in his plan of salvation by sending his Son into the world was, for all the obscurity of Jesus' birth, an enormously complex undertaking. It also tells me that in the midst of all the complexity, individuals have a part to play, because what they do always has an impact on the lives of others, however small, however slight. If modern chaos theory tells us that the fluttering of a butterfly's wings in the Brazilian rainforest can affect the weather on the other side of the world, then we have to conclude that all our actions contribute to the flow of history, and all our actions can contribute to the outworking of God's purposes.

As we follow the script by exploring the credit list, be encouraged. You are helping to write the next act of God's epic production.

15 December

CAESAR AUGUSTUS: THE ROMAN PEACE

In those days Caesar Augustus issued a decree that a census should be taken of the entire Roman world. (This was the first census that took place while Quirinius was governor of Syria.) And everyone went to his own town to register. So Joseph also went up from the town of Nazareth in Galilee to Judea, to Bethlehem the town of David, because he belonged to the house and line of David. He went there to register with Mary, who was pledged to be married to him and was expecting a child.

LUKE 2:1–5

It's just a brief mention—not even enough to make it on to that nativity play cast list. But he was the one with the power: he issued a decree and everyone did what they were told. These few verses link the biggest of big pictures with the intimate cameo of a couple about to become a family. They remind us of those film sequences that start with the globe and zoom in, and in, and in, until one individual is searched out and focused on full frame. They link the most powerful man in the world to an unborn child, the political centre of the known world with simple domesticity. They remind us that Joseph had something that was beyond the grasp even of the great Augustus: he came from a long royal line that was now without political power, but carried the promises of God.

Augustus is more Shakespeare play than nativity play. He was born in 63BC, named Octavius, his only link to power being the fact that his grandmother was the sister of Julius Caesar. He was still a teenager, just on the first rungs of the ladder of Roman politics, when

Julius Caesar was assassinated in 44BC. Two days later, Caesar's will revealed that Octavius was his adopted son and chief heir. Octavius renamed himself Julius Caesar Octavian, and within 18 months he had used his brilliant political skill, enormous nerve and terrifying ruthlessness to seize a share of power. The same qualities saw him emerge in 30BC as the sole leader of the Roman empire after the defeat and death of Mark Antony. Three years later, he renamed himself Caesar Augustus ('the exalted'), and continued to consolidate his power and control over his vast empire, which he ruled until his death in AD14.

Augustus was given the title of 'Father of the Country', the position of chief priest, the status of the son of a god, and the award of a crown as the saviour of lives. In his life he was worshipped by many, his will and essence recognized as divine; in death he was named as the 'divine Augustus'. The beginnings of the imperial cult struck at the heart of the claims made by Jesus and his followers. The language used by the New Testament letter writers to describe Jesus was language already being used about the Roman emperor: on the one hand, Christians saw the words and titles used in the political arena as representing the demand of Jesus for total allegiance; on the other hand, emperors were using religious concepts to reinforce their political power. It was not surprising that they came into conflict.

They did so in the context of the high point of Roman civilization, the period of stability and growth known as *pax romana*, the Roman peace. It is seen as the great achievement of Augustus, and made him arguably the single most important figure in Roman history. In establishing a new system for Roman government that was to stand for three centuries, he made possible the longest period of unity, peace and prosperity that western Europe, the Middle East and the north African seaboard have known in their entire recorded history.

The fact is that Jesus entered the world at the very moment when a whole range of factors were particularly conducive to the spread of a new religion. The Roman empire encompassed most of the known world, bridging east and west, providing an enormous geographical area linked together, with peace established and guaranteed after a hundred years of civil war by a professional and loyal standing army from Spain to the Danube, north Africa and Egypt to Arabia. Augustus maintained an honest government and a sound currency system, which encouraged growing trade among the provinces, facilitated by the new ease of communication.

The seas were made safe from pirates; the highway system connecting Rome with its far-flung empire was extended. This was a new age of travel: people and goods could move around more widely and more easily than ever before—and people could carry a new message. Augustus even developed an efficient postal service, well used later by Paul, sending all those epistles to keep in touch with the growing network of churches. His letters were written in the common language of the empire—not Latin, the language of the conquerors, but Greek, the language of ideas, of art, of commerce. The New Testament is written in this everyday Greek (*koine*), readily understood by many people in every nation.

Those people had a wide range of religious beliefs and practices. The characteristic Roman approach was to permit and absorb, a toleration that was practical in terms of keeping subject peoples happy, and recognized that political rather than religious factors were the cement that held the empire together. Christianity grew initially as a sect within Judaism, which was an acknowledged and permitted religion within the empire. It spread mainly through the network of Jewish communities, themselves already spread, before bursting out into the wider society and then coming into conflict with the authorities.

The empire had to be paid for. Taxation was as vital to the state then as now! And taxation required an accurate assessment of the population: hence the practice of registering and census taking. There is an ongoing debate among historians and commentators about the text, the dating and the texation process, trying to match Luke's account with other historical evidence. It's interesting stuff, but not conclusive. What is clear, though, is that Luke believed it was the hated taxation process of a foreign emperor that caused a pregnant young woman to head for Bethlehem, the town of David.

We all live our lives deeply affected by the geography, history, sociology and culture of our surroundings. We are shaped by these forces as they interplay with our genetic make-up and our upbringing.

Caesar Augustus shaped an entire world, but he did not control it. It was filled out with the lives of individuals, and for some of them God's Spirit was shaping their world even more powerfully. The 'Roman peace' lasted until AD180; the baby may have been born in an outhouse in a small village on the edge of the empire as a result of the emperor's decree, but that birth brought into being a new kingdom whose peace will last for ever. Augustus may have been named a god, but he was a poor substitute for the real thing. It was no contest.

Almighty God, King of kings, Lord of lords,
we recognize your power and authority.
You are greater than any individual;
you are greater than any forces of culture and society.
All will bow at your feet.
Release the power of your Spirit into our lives,
so that rather than being shaped by all the forces around us,
we can affect them, and see them conform to your kingdom.
Amen.

16 December

HEROD THE GREAT: MURDER AT CHRISTMAS

After Jesus was born in Bethlehem in Judea, during the time of King Herod, Magi from the east came to Jerusalem and asked, 'Where is the one who has been born king of the Jews? We saw his star in the east and have come to worship him.' When King Herod heard this he was disturbed, and all Jerusalem with him. When he had called together all the people's chief priests and teachers of the law, he asked them where the Christ was to be born. 'In Bethlehem in Judea,' they replied, 'for this is what the prophet has written: "But you, Bethlehem, in the land of Judah, are by no means least among the rulers of Judah; for out of you will come a ruler who will be the shepherd of my people Israel."'

Then Herod called the Magi secretly and found out from them the exact time the star had appeared. He sent them to Bethlehem and said, 'Go and make a careful search for the child. As soon as you find him, report to me, so that I too may go and worship him.' ...

When Herod realized that he had been outwitted by the Magi, he was furious, and he gave orders to kill all the boys in Bethlehem and its vicinity who were two years old and under, in accordance with the time he had learned from the Magi. Then what was said through the prophet Jeremiah was fulfilled: 'A voice is heard in Ramah, weeping and great mourning, Rachel weeping for her children and refusing to be comforted, because they are no more.'

MATTHEW 2:1–8, 16–18

King Herod is the pantomime villain of the nativity play: it is not unknown for him to be booed as he takes the stage! What's more, he had ten wives—and the first one was named Doris! I can't help feeling that this fact has not been exploited enough. It could add to the number of parts available for girls, for example, as well as offering opportunity for a comedy interlude—except that Herod's part in the story is not funny.

One of the key features of Augustus' reign was his use of lesser kings to rule parts of his empire. They were dependent on him for their power, but also a useful buffer between both the people and the detail of these specific areas. Herod the Great was one of these 'client-kings': he may have been named 'Great', but his greatness was definitely subject to Caesar's. He was half Jewish, his father being from the region of Idumea and his mother the daughter of an Arabian sheikh. He became governor of Galilee at the age of 16, and Mark Antony subsequently made him tetrarch of Galilee as Herod picked his way through the political minefield of imperial politics after the assassination of Julius Caesar. Eventually the Romans backed him with their legions and he established himself as the sole ruler of Judea in 37BC.

Herod's rule was marked by grandiose building programmes, designed partly to enhance his political power and his standing with the people. He began with new walls for Jerusalem and a citadel next to the temple. Then he provided a new market and a theatre, and began to rebuild the temple itself. At the same time, he built a new port, named Caesarea in honour of the emperor and including a temple where Augustus could be worshipped.

All these signs of growing prosperity did little to pacify his people, however. They resented being ruled by someone they regarded as non-Jewish, someone who readily identified with Greek ways rather than Jewish traditions, and was clearly supported by Roman power. The Roman eagle on the gate of the new temple, within which sacrifices were made twice a day on behalf of Augustus and the Roman people, was a highly contentious symbolic reminder of their subjugation. Herod's levels of taxation were excessive by the standards of the time, and were enforced by resort to violence and the secret police. His ten marriages only served to make him more unpopular.

His reign ended in violence and terror. In 8BC, Jewish teachers at the monastery in Qumran encouraged their pupils to remove the golden eagle from the temple—and, in retaliation, teachers and pupils were burned alive inside the monastery. Herod was now ill with an extremely unpleasant gangrenous disease, and anxious about a struggle for the succession within his family. As a result, in 7 and 4BC, he had two of his own sons executed in a grotesque attempt to control the future.

This was the highly charged situation into which the Magi appeared and announced that they were looking for one who was born 'King of the Jews'. The Magi may have been learned, but they must have been politically naive: it would have been hard to imagine a more explosive statement in Herod's court at that particular time. Their appearance must have dramatically increased the level of Herod's paranoia, which makes his reaction perhaps a little more understandable, if no less inexcusable. If he was prepared to murder his own sons, then he was clearly capable of wreaking havoc on the lives of others by wholesale slaughter.

One of the highlights of my elder daughter's career at university was a small but startlingly dramatic appearance in the York Mystery Plays. These medieval pageants, dramatizations of the Bible story, were undoubtedly a forerunner of the nativity play tradition. In York, a selection of the 48 plays within the cycle is performed every four years, and Katharine was thrilled to get a part. She was a 'Herod heavy' (cast against character, I must assure you). The family dutifully gathered, took their seats, and watched as Katharine and her colleagues, complete with calf-high Doc Martens, re-enacted the massacre of the innocents. It was stunningly effective. The audience almost held its breath as red ribbons imitated the bloody reality of sudden death.

This is not the Christmas story depicted on the colourful cards on the mantelpiece. It is not the saccharine sweetness of fresh, clean straw and spotless mangers. It is the vicious, ruthless reality of power politics, and it is hard to stomach. It should not be part of the story—but it is. It intrudes into the escapist fantasy of the traditional Christmas like an unpleasant and unwelcome guest.

To that extent, it is perhaps a healthy reality check. Jesus was born into a real world of violence and suffering: indeed, that was the reality that made him 'leave his throne and his kingly crown' to come to earth, as the carol puts it. That same reality brutally interrupted the Christmas celebrations when the giant tsunami waves devastated the coastal communities of South Asia on Boxing Day 2004. Christmas is not an invitation to pretend for a few days that all is right with the world. It is an opportunity to remember that God is so deeply affected by human pain and human inhumanity that he was prepared to take on human form, to bear that same pain and inhumanity himself and begin an intervention that leads, slowly and inexorably, to the promised time and place where there will be no more suffering, no more tears.

There were tears in Bethlehem that first Christmas. It is hard to understand why the moment of hope, planned and foreseen for centuries, from before time itself, should result in the death of these tiny babies. The only conclusion I can draw is that Herod's monstrous crime somehow reflects and symbolizes the response of evil to the act of divine love—and that it should reinforce the determination of the followers of Jesus to protect children and to resist tyranny. Innocents are still being massacred, by poverty as well as by political violence. Innocence is being massacred by child pornography and child abuse. True celebration of Christmas should never drown out the sound of mothers weeping for their children.

Jesus, born at Christmas and raised as a child,
hear our cry for children in danger
and for the mothers who weep. Amen.

SHEPHERDS: THE CHOSEN WITNESSES

And there were shepherds living out in the fields nearby, keeping watch over their flocks at night. An angel of the Lord appeared to them, and the glory of the Lord shone around them, and they were terrified. But the angel said to them, 'Do not be afraid. I bring you good news of great joy that will be for all the people. Today in the town of David a Saviour has been born to you; he is Christ the Lord. This will be a sign to you: You will find a baby wrapped in cloths and lying in a manger.' Suddenly a great company of the heavenly host appeared with the angel, praising God and saying, 'Glory to God in the highest, and on earth peace to those on whom his favour rests.'

When the angels had left them and gone into heaven, the shepherds said to one another, 'Let's go to Bethlehem and see this thing that has happened, which the Lord has told us about.' So they hurried off and found Mary and Joseph, and the baby, who was lying in the manger. When they had seen him, they spread the word concerning what had been told them about this child, and all who heard it were amazed at what the shepherds said to them. But Mary treasured up all these things and pondered them in her heart. The shepherds returned, glorifying and praising God for all the things they had heard and seen, which were just as they had been told.

LUKE 2:8–20

From emperors and kings to shepherds: there could scarcely be a greater contrast. Herod pretended he wanted to worship; the shepherds really did worship. For all their power, their secret police and informers, neither Augustus nor Herod was given the information that the shepherds received. The angel messengers appeared in the regal splendour of the night sky rather than the palaces of Rome or Jerusalem.

Luke, in his Gospel, delights that Jesus touches the lives of the untouchables, those outside the fold of political power or religious prestige—whether they are people who are poor, children, widows, the sick, those with mental illness, Gentiles, women, or even Gentile women. Right at the start of the story, while Jesus is no more than a few hours old, it is shepherds who are chosen to witness the birth of the Christ-child.

'Witness' is an interesting word. Shepherds were not regarded as reliable witnesses, not allowed to give evidence in court at all, such was the contempt in which they were held by Jewish society of the time. They were at the bottom of the heap, a position they shared with traitorous tax collectors and street cleaners: they were labelled 'sinners'. The Mishnah, the record of the oral traditions of the Jewish rabbis, describes shepherds as being 'incompetent' and suggests that there was no obligation to rescue a shepherd who had fallen into a pit. To buy wool, milk or a kid from a shepherd was forbidden, on the assumption that it would be stolen property.

This seems strange. After all, the patriarchs had essentially been shepherds, and many Eastern peoples referred to their kings as 'shepherds'. But it seems that attitudes perhaps first learned in Egypt, where shepherds were despised ('all shepherds are detestable to the Egyptians', Genesis 46:34), were taken up in the promised land, where the wandering herders of the exodus largely became agriculturalists. Also, of course, the Bible records a long history of tension between crop growers and herdsmen (sheep and goats tend to eat and damage crops), which began with Cain and Abel.

Yet the great King David had begun his career as a shepherd. He wrote a psalm which drew on that experience (Psalm 23, 'The Lord is my shepherd'), but the rabbis are said to have asked with amazement how, in view of the despicable nature of shepherds, God could possibly be compared to one. Nevertheless, God not only revealed himself to them, making them the first witnesses of the birth of Jesus; Jesus also said that they were among the very group he had come for: 'I have not come to call the righteous, but sinners' (Mark 2:17). And he announced himself as 'the good shepherd' who lays down his life for the sheep (John 10:11), in contrast to the thieves and hired shepherds. He was the one 'who will be like a shepherd for my people Israel' (Matthew 2:6, CEV).

The angels' appearance to the shepherds was not only a sign of a new beginning, a turning point in human history. It also indicated a crucial feature of this new 'upside-down' kingdom: its citizens would be those who are used to being excluded. Doors so long bolted shut would be forced open by the Messiah who had no social or racial prejudice.

The shepherds were living out in the fields, 'keeping watch'. Close to Bethlehem, on the road to Jerusalem, was a tower known as Migdal Eder, which means 'the watch-tower of the flock'. The tradition was that, here, shepherds watched over the flocks destined to be sacrifices in the temple. Perhaps John the Baptist was not the first to recognize 'the Lamb of God, who takes away the sin of the world' (John 1:29). Certainly they left the stable and 'spread the word concerning what had been told them about this child' (Luke 2:17).

Whom did they tell? Did they go back to the fields and tell the sheep? Or did they take the flocks on down to Jerusalem, and tell everyone they met in the course of doing their business? Perhaps there was a greater purpose to the selection of the shepherds as the first witnesses. They would have taken the news of the Messiah, Christ the Lord, to the very heart of the place where the most hopeful and expectant would gather. That group would have included Simeon and Anna: perhaps they were watching and waiting when Mary and Joseph brought the baby into the temple as the law required.

This is supposition, of course, but it does make sense of the gap between the shepherds spreading the word in verse 17 and returning, glorifying and praising God, in verse 20. It is just possible that it was from the temple that they returned to their homes, their duties done and their experience enriched. So it is supposition based on historical fact and on a positive interpretation of the purposes of God.

The coming of Jesus is a sign of God's love for his world. The circumstances of his birth recorded by the Gospel writers are an indication of the nature of that love, and its transforming power. Here the good news is revealed to the despised shepherds; two thousand years later, the church honours its ministers with the title of 'pastor', as shepherds who care for their flocks of God's people.

Across the world, the gospel of Jesus has a special appeal for the despised, the excluded and the poor—from the *dalits*, the 'untouchables' of India, to the tribal peoples of South Asia; from the indigenous Indians of Latin America to the shanty-town dwellers of some of the biggest cities in the world; from prisoners in jail to European gypsy communities. They join the shepherds in worship of the Christ, because they know that he is the one who stands with those on the outside of society and brings them to the centre of his kingdom. Thus, this kingdom is not an easy place for the snobbish: God's arms are outstretched to those who are used to seeing noses turned up. This is a special challenge to the churches of the wealthy. Are the 'shepherds' of our own society only to be allowed into the nativity play, or will they be welcomed around the communion table?

You are the God of the outcast,
the God who gives sinners a seat at the banquet.
We praise you for those cast out by their society
who are finding a welcome from you.
Good Lord, save your church from snobbery and prejudice;
help us all to be as welcoming as you are to all,
regardless of standing or reputation. Amen.

18 December

MAGI: WRITTEN IN THE STARS

After Jesus was born in Bethlehem in Judea, during the time of King Herod, Magi from the east came to Jerusalem and asked, 'Where is the one who has been born king of the Jews? We saw his star in the east and have come to worship him.' ...

They went on their way, and the star they had seen in the east went ahead of them until it stopped over the place where the child was. When they saw the star, they were overjoyed. On coming to the house, they saw the child with his mother Mary, and they bowed down and worshipped him. Then they opened their treasures and presented him with gifts of gold and of incense and of myrrh.

MATTHEW 2:1–2, 9–11

Magi is the plural of 'magus', a word that originally meant an ancient Persian priest. In the book of Daniel, the word is used for the wise men who interpreted dreams though astrology. By the time of the New Testament, it referred to anyone who used magic arts—arguably among those you would most want to keep away from a baby. But then, God's ways are not our ways.

It is hard to read these familiar verses without thinking of little children in cardboard crowns and adapted curtains, or even the oft-sung carol that seems to lend itself to the varied words which amuse the same little children. I grew up in Birmingham, convinced that nearby suburb Perry Barr was an integral part of the Christmas story ('one on a scooter, blowing his hooter, going to Perry Barr'—sorry to have to spell it out).

The same carol precipitates a traditional Christmas debate: were there really three kings? The Bible never calls them kings and never specifies how many there were. It certainly never mentions Melchior, Caspar or Balthazar. We don't know whether they were all men, whether there were three or twelve. We do know that the story sits, however sparse in detail, at the beginning of Matthew's Gospel, an exotic insert into an already extraordinary story—arguably so strange that it could hardly be made up.

Behind the nativity play trivialization, however, there is a story with profound implications. The moment of God's intervention in human history had such cosmic significance that it was written in the stars; it had such universal significance that it was revealed to people far removed from all hint of God's revelation thus far.

I have a vivid memory of gazing at the stars. I was in a remote part of Paraguay in South America, more than 200 miles from the nearest electric light, with nothing to detract from the diamond-like brilliance of starlight, pin-pricked across the inky-black night sky. I discovered why the Milky Way is so named—a brushstroke of pale and delicate luminescence, startling in its breadth and clarity.

I can also recall a visit to the Planetarium, the awesome facts of space almost overwhelming the technological skill that revealed the ever-changing movement of the planets—ever changing but, of course, predictable. Some of us look at the stars and think of romance; some search for meaning. The ancient astrologers were convinced that constant, careful star-gazing would enable them to detect the variations on the predictable that would then demand interpretation. They had no computers, no experience of space travel, but they had perseverance and they had conviction.

God's purpose expressed in the birth of Jesus was a plan designed to impact the whole of the creation. Not only were 'all things created by him and for him', but 'God was pleased... through him to reconcile to himself all things, whether things on earth or things in heaven, by making peace through his blood, shed on the cross' (Colossians 1:16, 19–20). The *shalom* of the universe was to be restored; is it any wonder that the first sign of this cosmic change was revealed in the stars? At the moment of his death, the earth shook (Matthew 27:51); at the moment of his birth, the heavens were telling the glory of God, the skies proclaiming the work of his hands (Psalm 19:1).

The magi, as a result of their diligence, knew that the time was right. As *The Message* puts it, trying to capture the flavour of the moment, 'They could hardly contain themselves: They were in the right place! They had arrived at the right time!' (Matthew 2:10). The time was right for the birth of a king. The time was right for the Jewish people to receive a new king, the one through whom all nations would be blessed. The time was right for the magi to act upon what they had seen. Not for them the simple self-satisfaction of knowledge gained. They did not know or understand the full story. God's plan was revealed to them, but not in detail. Yet they knew enough to realize that they had to move towards the centre of God's purpose; they had to meet the king.

It is tragic that so many people catch a glimpse of God, but turn their backs and stay put. Churchgoers can fill their heads with more knowledge about Jesus than the magi could ever have thought possible, but not all have the courage to set out on the rollercoaster of discovery that is the journey of faith. The clichéd Christmas poster contains a truth, despite the cheesiness of the sentiment: wise men (and women) do still seek Jesus. And seeking requires movement—of mind and spirit, if not always of body.

For the magi, it meant a willingness to ask awkward questions of a tyrant and a willingness to bow the knee to a baby. Whether in the imposing grandeur of a palace or amid the earthy aroma of a stable, they had the courage, perseverance and humility required to complete the journey.

The magi perceived a message of great significance and acted upon it. They travelled afar. They appear incongruously alongside the shepherds, distant star-gazers rubbing shoulders with the local farmhands, their common experience a revelation in the sky that had led them to the stable. Their coming was a sign to all, and a reminder to us, that God's purposes in sending Jesus extended far beyond the confines of one nationality or geographical area. The gospel is for all nationalities, all nations.

This story is also a reminder that God has his own special means of communication. Right now, in the very lands that were home to the magi, God is speaking in dreams that encourage people to seek and to find the same Jesus. It is one of the great and exciting mysteries of our time, but no more than an indication that God moves in his own way to fulfil his purposes.

Take a look at that nativity scene arranged in your hearth or on the mantelpiece. The magi are there because the king they sought and found was, and is, the king of all creation, of all peoples in every place. Their presence is a sign that you have every right to be there as well, kneeling in worship before the baby who changed the world.

God, whose greatness is revealed in the heavens,
grant us the insight to know when we should move
in response to the prompting of your Spirit,
and the courage to persevere in our journey with you. Amen.

19 December

ANGELS: PROPHESYING, PROTECTING, PRAISING

While Joseph was thinking about this, an angel from the Lord came to him in a dream. The angel said, 'Joseph, the baby that Mary will have is from the Holy Spirit. Go ahead and marry her. Then after her baby is born, name him Jesus, because he will save his people from their sins.' So the Lord's promise came true, just as the prophet had said, 'A virgin will have a baby boy, and he will be called Immanuel,' which means 'God is with us.'
MATTHEW 1:20–23 (CEV)

After the wise men had gone, an angel from the Lord appeared to Joseph in a dream and said, 'Get up! Hurry and take the child and his mother to Egypt! Stay there until I tell you to return, because Herod is looking for the child and wants to kill him.' That night, Joseph got up and took his wife and the child to Egypt, where they stayed until Herod died. So the Lord's promise came true, just as the prophet had said, 'I called my son out of Egypt.'
MATTHEW 2:13–15 (CEV)

All at once an angel came down to them from the Lord, and the brightness of the Lord's glory flashed around them. The shepherds were frightened. But the angel said, 'Don't be afraid! I have good news for you, which will make everyone happy. This very day in King David's home town a Saviour was born for you. He is Christ the Lord. You will know who he is, because you will find him dressed in baby clothes and lying on a bed of hay.' Suddenly many other angels came down from heaven and joined in praising God. They said: 'Praise God in heaven! Peace on earth to everyone who pleases God.'
LUKE 2:9–14 (CEV)

I wonder what you think about angels? There could be all sorts of possibilities. You may believe in angels, or you may be sceptical. Surveys tell us that a US citizen is far more likely to believe in angels than a UK citizen, which is perhaps a sign of how much more secularized British society has become, and how much that has affected the church.

I will confess that I have come across angels in only three places: as the winner of the 'best costume' award in nativity plays, in second-hand bookshops, which clearly only qualify as well-stocked when they include a copy of Billy Graham's book *Angels*, and in popular culture, where (in films and on television) angels appear surprisingly frequently, as a kind of good fairy intervening to spread a little light and happiness into otherwise miserable situations. To some people, therefore, their role in the Christmas story is no more than a reminder of the fairy-tale unreality of the season, while to others it is a sign and a confirmation of the spiritually cosmic significance of God's intervention in human history. The incarnation—'Our God contracted to a span, incomprehensibly made Man', as Charles Wesley put it—was a once-in-eternity event, and drew on spiritual resources rarely needed so powerfully before or since.

Who are we dealing with here? Angels as revealed in the Bible are spiritual beings, created by God, worshipping God in the heavenly places, yet capable of sin—and visible to human beings only when God chooses, usually to carry out specific tasks. They are an interface between the physical world and the spiritual world, which is just as real but not discerned with the physical senses. I love the story of Elisha's servant, who wakes up one morning to discover that he and his master are surrounded by hostile forces. Elisha prays that his eyes will be opened, so the servant makes an even more important discovery: not just that the hills are full of horses and chariots of fire all around Elisha, but that 'those who are with us are more than those who are with them' (2 Kings 6:16).

This was the kind of reassurance that the angel brought to Joseph. What kind of messenger would you have needed in his situation? Joseph was struggling to match his knowledge of the nature of the young woman chosen to be his wife with the news of her pregnancy. His mind was in a turmoil of doubt and indecision, which was ended by the authority of the word that the angel brought in his dream. This was not an empty gesture of encouragement. It was a direct statement of the fact of God's intervention, and an explanation of its purpose. Jesus would 'save his people from their sins'. The Bible indicates that this is an act of God which is appreciated by angels ('there is joy before the angels of God over one sinner that repents', Luke 15:10, RSV), even though they themselves cannot enter into the experience: 'Since the children have flesh and blood, he too shared in their humanity so that by his death he might destroy him who holds the power of death—that is, the devil—and free those who all their lives were held in slavery by their fear of death. For surely it is not angels he helps, but Abraham's descendants' (Hebrews 2:14–16).

Prophecy is never an end in itself: it is the word of God, intended to have an impact on the hearer. Joseph was entrusted with the big picture of God's plan and purpose by this divine intervention, and it gave him the encouragement to go on and play his part. Then, with the baby born, there came another dream—and this time a warning. This was a true guardian angel. It was another sign of God's plan at work: the life of the baby was preserved, and prophecy was fulfilled.

Over the fields of Bethlehem, the earthly skies were split open with a glimpse of the glory of heaven. 'Suddenly'—it was as if the message of the one angel triggered the opening of the floodgates of praise from the multitude of the heavenly host. I get goosebumps every time I hear a choir let rip with Handel's 'Hallelujah Chorus', but this was the greatest choir the world has ever heard, a private performance for a tiny group of privileged shepherds. They discovered that the worship of heaven was directly linked to God's activity on earth—activity that is all about peace, the restoration of the *shalom* destroyed by sin.

The Christmas angels remind us that the coming of Jesus is a deeply powerful spiritual event. The very fact that history is dated either BC or AD signifies that this is the pivotal moment in the story of the human race. Perhaps this Christmas could be a pivotal moment in our own personal history: make sure you are listening for the sounds of heaven above the muzak and the jangling cash-tills.

We hear the Christmas angels
The great glad tidings tell.
O come to us, abide with us,
Our Lord Emmanuel.

20 December

TEACHERS OF THE LAW: MASTERS OF THE REFERENCE LIBRARY

After Jesus was born in Bethlehem in Judea, during the time of King Herod, Magi from the east came to Jerusalem and asked, 'Where is the one who has been born king of the Jews? We saw his star in the east and have come to worship him.' When King Herod heard this he was disturbed, and all Jerusalem with him. When he had called together all the people's chief priests and teachers of the law, he asked them where the Christ was to be born. 'In Bethlehem in Judea,' they replied, 'for this is what the prophet has written: "But you, Bethlehem, in the land of Judah, are by no means least among the rulers of Judah; for out of you will come a ruler who will be the shepherd of my people Israel.'

Then Herod called the Magi secretly and found out from them the exact time the star had appeared. He sent them to Bethlehem and said, 'Go and make a careful search for the child. As soon as you find him, report to me, so that I too may go and worship him.'

MATTHEW 2:1–8

I love reference libraries. My local library has a reference section where I pore over the *Which?* magazines when contemplating a significant purchase. Some people find it confusing (and my wife infuriating) that I head to the library when I want to buy a vacuum cleaner. One of my very favourite buildings in London is the Reading Room of the British Museum. I once did some research there, and I was so conscious of the ghosts of Karl Marx and the many other famous writers who had sat within its walls, thinking great thoughts, that very little work was done. Now we always take visitors to

London to see it in all its restored glory, a Victorian temple to learning—and I check to see if my name has been added to the list of famous ticket-holders!

I have never been completely convinced that skill in using a reference library is regarded as of significant value in our society. Occasionally, people have mooted the idea of a church skill-share scheme, by which each person shares with others their particular skill. I think they are a great idea: a plumber offers time and is repaid by the electrician; the gardener sorts out the flowerbeds, and in return calls on the accountant to help with the income tax return. But somehow, offering to look something up in a book doesn't seem quite to cut the mustard!

When the magi created a stunned silence in Herod's court by a simple but politically explosive request for information, Herod was very sure that he valued the academic approach. There were two competing groups of religious authorities in his kingdom: the chief priests, largely concerned with the formal rituals of the temple, and the scribes, or teachers of the law. This latter group emphasized the oral tradition of the law, and had built a job for themselves through the need to teach their extremely complex interpretations and detailed rules. The question about the birthplace of the Christ, however, was so important that their rivalry was ignored. Every available scholar was called in: suddenly their books mattered and their knowledge counted. But there was no need to scurry to the library or even 'phone a friend'. They knew the answer straight away. It was a straightforward starter for ten, and they pressed their buzzers without delay.

The question was not difficult. Those who were looking to God to keep his promise and send a Messiah who would rescue his people from their captivity had scoured the prophets' writings, looking for the clues that would tell them when the right moment and the right man had come. And one of the clearest clues came in Micah 5:2. 'But you, Bethlehem Ephrathah, though you are small among the clans of Judah, out of you will come for me one who will be ruler over Israel, whose origins are from of old, from ancient times.' (Note that Matthew 2:6 quotes from the Septuagint, the Greek translation of the Old Testament produced between 300 and 200BC and widely used at the time of Christ.)

Micah was a contemporary of Isaiah, writing around the time of King Hezekiah. Israel was divided and facing disaster. The prophet looks forward to a time when the nation would be reunited. At the same time, though, he refers back, seeing the future in the light of the past: the origins of this ruler are from ancient times. Matthew's family tree is an echo of this promise, as he sets out the generational links down through human history. In fact, Micah's original Hebrew suggests the reality we have been considering—that the origins of Jesus are not just in the ancient line of David, but stretch back into eternity itself. The CEV translation of Micah 5:2 reads, 'someone whose family goes back to ancient times', while the footnote suggests an alternative reading of 'someone whose kingdom is eternal'. It could be emphasizing that the Messiah would come from God; it could be indicating that the advent of the Messiah was planned long ago in the purposes of God.

Micah also gave a prophetic indication of when this would happen and what it would mean: 'The Lord will abandon Israel only until this ruler is born, and the rest of his family returns to Israel. Like a shepherd taking care of his sheep, this ruler will lead and care for his people by the power and glorious name of the Lord his God. His people will live securely, and the whole earth will know his true greatness, because he will bring peace' (Micah 5:3–5, CEV). He was looking to a period when the exile had ended, which would be characterized by peace, the *shalom* of God, known across the world.

Micah made this prophecy completely against the grain of history. The line of David had already been humiliated and defeated when he was writing. Seven hundred years later, things had only got worse, and all that remained was God's promise. Herod's scholars knew the answer to the question—but did they believe it would ever happen?

Herod believed them. He got the answer and he acted upon it. To that extent, his is a good pattern to follow. The Bible has the answer to many questions, but they are not there for academic consideration or simply intellectual stimulation. God wants us to act upon them, in line with his law and his love. That was Herod's mistake: his action was devious and his intention murderous. Little did the scholars know how much would ride on their answer.

God, you are the source of all knowledge;
give us enquiring minds to search out your truth.
God, you spoke and it was done;
give us willing hearts to act on your truth.
Amen.

21 December

LUKE: AN ORDERLY ACCOUNT

Many have undertaken to draw up an account of the things that have been fulfilled among us, just as they were handed down to us by those who from the first were eyewitnesses and servants of the word. Therefore, since I myself have carefully investigated everything from the beginning, it seemed good also to me to write an orderly account for you, most excellent Theophilus, so that you may know the certainty of the things you have been taught.

LUKE 1:1–4

I used to be a historian. I always think that makes me sound quite grand. Someone once told me that I should not use the past tense—once a historian, always a historian, they argued. But the truth was that I studied it and taught it, but I never wrote any history. I feel that if I had actually written a history book, then I really could claim to be a historian.

Luke was a historian. He may have been an amateur, he may have lacked a university degree, but the writings of Doctor Luke have become the most widely read history books in the world, not least because of the significance of their subject.

In the course of my studies, I read many history books, so I can claim to have some insight, on the basis of experience, into what makes for good historical writing. My two favourite history books highlight the essential qualities. *The Siege of Malta* is Ernle Bradford's riveting account of an extraordinary event of the 16th century, a story to equal any thriller, told with consummate skill, and with the vital extra ingredient: the story is true. George Dangerfield's *The Strange Death of Liberal England* covers a less exotic but equally dramatic period, the last decade before World War I. It is full of fascinating insights, analysis that stimulates thoughtfulness, and a new understanding of the significance of events. It also takes seriously the role of ordinary people in making history.

These are exactly the qualities displayed by both the biblical historians who include the Christmas story in their narratives. They are dealing with the ultimate extraordinary event of human history, the moment when, as John puts it, 'the Word became flesh' (John 1:14). Their accounts are full of fascinating insights, and both take seriously the role of ordinary people in making history—whether carpenters, astrologers or shepherds.

Even more important, they are writing history to stimulate thoughtfulness and encourage understanding. It is a common misunderstanding that history is simply a collection of facts. Of course, to be genuine history, to be good history, there has to be a careful marshalling of fact with no deviation from truth; but all history offers a selection of facts, chosen according to the writer's values and beliefs and designed to offer an explanation of the significance of events and to discern a pattern of meaning.

Many people in our world dismiss the Gospels as propaganda, not history. The difference is important. It lies entirely in the attitude to truth. Propaganda is indifferent to the truth of the facts presented, and manipulates them shamelessly, perverting the truth ruthlessly in pursuit of its goals. History not only limits itself to dealing with verifiable facts, but is committed to using them to illuminate truth, not to ignore or distort it.

It's worth pausing and asking what our own attitude is to truth. Christians tend to assume that because we all know lying is wrong, then that's the matter dealt with. We live in a world dominated by voices that want to persuade us to take their advice, buy their product, vote for them at an election—and most of us are confident that we have a healthy scepticism about such persuaders. We believe that we are well able to sift the wheat from the chaff of the information we receive.

We have to beware, however, of the one extreme, where we

become sceptical of anyone's ability to tell us the truth, and the other extreme, where we are all too ready to believe some sources rather than others. I tend to believe my newspaper of choice, my politician of choice—even my pastor and preacher of choice—more than the others.

Christians also are in the business of persuasion. We love to see people come to faith, and the danger is that we may love it so much, we are willing to cut corners to get there. A bit of exaggeration here, leaving out a detail there—it is all too easily done. Let's be clear: when Paul wrote, 'I have become all things to all people so that by all possible means I might save some' (1 Corinthians 9:22), he was not including the possibility of distorting the truth for the sake of the gospel.

At the time of the Iraq war, there was much concern about the extent to which information had been 'sexed up' to justify going to war. Yet Christians will make all sort of advertising claims for their events: even church notices can see the effort to create enthusiasm overspill into unjustifiable hyperbole, stretching the truth to the limit. It matters. People find it very easy to extend their cynicism about politicians to religious people who are revealed to be willing to stretch the truth to market their gospel—and thus the whole witness of the church is damaged.

When Jesus said to Pontius Pilate, 'Everyone who cares for truth, who has any feeling for the truth, recognizes my voice', Pilate replied, 'What is truth?' (John 18:37–38, *The Message*). It was the verbal equivalent of the washing of his hands—more a weary, worldly-wise scepticism than a genuine philosophical concern, we suspect.

Luke has no such doubts. He begins his Gospel by making the purpose of his history quite explicit: he wants to offer his reader certainty. Right back in the beginning of the Christian era, there was the recognition that historical truth was vital. Peter agreed: 'When we told you about the power and the return of our Lord Jesus Christ, we were not telling clever stories that someone had made up. But with our own eyes we saw his true greatness' (2 Peter 1:16, CEV).

Paul knew what was at stake: 'If Christ wasn't raised to life, our message is worthless, and so is your faith. If the dead won't be raised to life, we have told lies about God by saying that he raised Christ to life, when he really did not' (1 Corinthians 15:14–15, CEV). Both Peter and Paul died as martyrs because what they believed was based on objective truth, not, in the words of the KJV translation of 2 Peter 1:16, 'cunningly devised fables'.

I was studying history at university when I had to decide whether or not I would believe for myself the faith I had been taught by my parents. I knew that if I believed it, I had to live by it, so there was a real temptation for me to cast off the constraints that, I believed, stemmed from trying to live as a Christian. But I could not escape the historical logic: if the resurrection had really happened, then everything else fell into place. It did not require an irrational leap of faith. The faith required was the faith needed to live by it.

Peter had seen with his own eyes. For Luke, his claim to certainty came from his careful investigations of the stories from eyewitnesses, and he wrote what he wrote because he wanted belief to be rooted in the reality of history. As John wrote, in conclusion to his Gosple, 'Jesus did many other miraculous signs in the presence of his disciples, which are not recorded in this book. But these are written that you may believe that Jesus is the Christ, the Son of God, and that by believing you may have life in his name' (John 20:30–31).

God of history, help us to learn the lessons of history.
God of truth, guard our lips that we may be people of truth.
God of the future, nourish the faith that leads to life eternal.
Amen.

22–28 DECEMBER

FAMILY AND FRIENDS

INTRODUCTION

The day is getting closer. There are very few windows left to open on your Advent calendar. It's time to focus in on those closest to the action. Families are always interesting when you know the members well. There are backbone characters, the ones who hold the family together. There are the eccentrics, whom everybody loves but probably prefers to take in small doses. (My wife Susan is an honorary 'mad auntie' to one family of children, who obviously felt they had no blood relation with quite the right qualifications.) There are the old, with all their memories, their awareness of the family history, which can be fascinating and even sometimes embarrassing. There are the young, developing their own unique role in the world in the context of their family upbringing and relationships.

Some families function well; others are, in modern parlance, dysfunctional—stifling cages from which their members long to break out. What clues can we glean from the biblical record about the family of Jesus? We can observe that they were religious. There were some people with religion as their profession, but the overwhelming impression is that this family did not go through the motions of religious observance out of tradition or without conviction. They had a lively faith. They were people who were looking for God to act, and willing to listen when he spoke to them. When he did so miraculously, they were fearful but not surprised or unbelieving. And they loved to worship, more than one of them bursting into song as they reflected on God's grace shown to them.

It is often said that you can't choose your family. But God did, and this is the family he chose. It was a significant choice. They were an ordinary family, made extraordinary. One minute, there was an older childless couple, and a middle-aged carpenter with a young fiancée, people who would scarcely have been given a second glance. Next, there are miracle babies on the way, their lives are changed for ever and their names will be known for ever. When Jesus is brought to his Father's house for the first time, there are two people who have the divine insight to see, in the lives of this family, a miracle long anticipated and long hoped for—a mark of God's blessing.

The wedding service reminds us that families are God's way of doing things: a place for human relationships to be affirmed and developed, a place of nurture and protection, a place of security and warmth. Christmas is a time for family, but all too often it is a time for families to experience stress and disharmony rather than blessing. Pray that God will be at work this Christmas, just as he was when the angels sang of peace all those years ago.

22 December

ZECHARIAH: LOST FOR WORDS

In the time of Herod king of Judea there was a priest named Zechariah, who belonged to the priestly division of Abijah; his wife Elizabeth was also a descendant of Aaron. Both of them were upright in the sight of God, observing all the Lord's commandments and regulations blamelessly. But they had no children, because Elizabeth was barren; and they were both well on in years.

Once when Zechariah's division was on duty and he was serving as priest before God, he was chosen by lot, according to the custom of the priesthood, to go into the temple of the Lord and burn incense. And when the time for the burning of incense came, all the assembled worshippers were praying outside.

Then an angel of the Lord appeared to him, standing at the right side of the altar of incense. When Zechariah saw him, he was startled and was gripped with fear. But the angel said to him: 'Do not be afraid, Zechariah; your prayer has been heard. Your wife Elizabeth will bear you a son, and you are to give him the name John. He will be a joy and delight to you, and many will rejoice because of his birth, for he will be great in the sight of the Lord. He is never to take wine or other fermented drink, and he will be filled with the Holy Spirit even from birth. Many of the people of Israel will he bring back to the Lord their God. And he will go on before the Lord, in the spirit and power of Elijah, to turn the hearts of the fathers to their children and the disobedient to the wisdom of the righteous—to make ready a people prepared for the Lord.'

Zechariah asked the angel, 'How can I be sure of this? I am an old man and my wife is well on in years.' The angel answered, 'I am Gabriel. I stand in the presence of God, and I have been sent to speak to you and to tell you this good news.'

LUKE 1:5–19

Sometimes our lives change gradually: one day we realize that things are not as they were, but we can't pin down any particular moment as being significant. Other times, something happens and our lives are changed for ever. When you speak to people about how they became a Christian, you hear both stories: some tell of a gradual process, in which they had a growing awareness of God and discovered that they had become followers of Jesus; others can name the place and the date, just like Paul on the Damascus road. In the Alpha course, Nicky Gumbel likens it to travelling on a train across Europe from Germany to France. During the day, you may see the border and know the exact moment when you entered a new country; at night, in the sleeping compartment, you have no idea when the border was crossed, but you wake up in Paris and you are just as sure that you have left one country and arrived in another.

Zechariah's life was changed on one day. It came late in life: he was at least 60 years old. It came on what was already a unique and special occasion. Zechariah was a priest, but not just any priest. There were two kinds of religious 'professionals' at this time. There were priests and Levites—and the priests were slightly superior because they were descended not only from Levi but also from Aaron. Zechariah was married to Elizabeth, who had the same ancestry, and this made Zechariah doubly honoured—except that Elizabeth had been unable to have children, and the honour had become a source of shame.

Priests had a special role in the temple: they were divided into 24 groups, and twice a year each group would be on duty in the temple. On this occasion, Zechariah is chosen, by the casting of lots, to burn incense on the altar of incense in the Holy Place. It was a great honour, and unique: once you had been chosen, you were never eligible for the choice again. Zechariah's task was to place the incense, representing the prayers of the people, on the heated altar, and then to lie prostrate in prayer. He would have been able to hear the people outside reciting their prayer: 'May the merciful God enter the Holy Place and accept with favour the offering of his people.' And at that moment, the pinnacle of Zechariah's career, that prayer was answered by the appearance of the angel from God.

One of the results of the coming of Jesus is that he has made it possible for us to enter his Holy Place, not just once, but whenever we wish—and yet we often lack the sense of privilege and thankfulness to take advantage of the incredible opportunity offered. And when we do enter, how expectant are we? Do we think that God might turn up in power? I suspect that if he did, many of us would be just as frightened as Zechariah was. Of course, we know that God is present when we meet together for worship: he has promised to be there. But we should praise God for the times when the worship takes us into his presence in a special way and we hear from him. So many people are disappointed and frustrated with their experience of church, and so many have no expectation of God on a Sunday morning—except, perhaps, that he will always be a gentleman and refrain from rocking the comforting boat of tradition and custom.

Zechariah was prostrate before God, and from this position he heard that God's impact on his life was not to be held within the walls of the temple. He and Elizabeth were to be granted their greatest wish: a son. He reacted with understandable amazement—and was rendered speechless. It meant a dramatic end to a dramatic moment. Zechariah was supposed to come out from the Holy Place to reassure the people that he had not been struck dead in God's presence, and then pronounce Aaron's high-priestly blessing over the people. The delay made the people nervous; then there was relief when he appeared, followed by the realization that something significant had happened, which had left him speechless.

He wasn't speechless when John the Baptist was born, though. Zechariah had been patient for nine months. Now worship, thankfulness and praise poured out. It's not an uncommon reaction for new fathers—and this was a father who knew that God had intervened miraculously and generously in his life. As Luke tells us:

Zechariah was filled with the Holy Spirit and prophesied:

'Praise be to the Lord, the God of Israel, because he has come and has redeemed his people. He has raised up a horn of salvation for us in the

house of his servant David (as he said through his holy prophets of long ago), salvation from our enemies and from the hand of all who hate us—to show mercy to our fathers and to remember his holy covenant, the oath he swore to our father Abraham: to rescue us from the hand of our enemies, and to enable us to serve him without fear in holiness and righteousness before him all our days.

'And you, my child, will be called a prophet of the Most High; for you will go on before the Lord to prepare the way for him, to give his people the knowledge of salvation through the forgiveness of their sins, because of the tender mercy of our God, by which the rising sun will come to us from heaven to shine on those living in darkness and in the shadow of death, to guide our feet into the path of peace.'

LUKE 1:67–79

Zechariah rejoiced not just because God had kept his promise to him, but because he recognized that the promises of God to his people from long ago were now being fulfilled. This was not a parochial prayer focused on himself; this was a big-picture prayer, a paean of praise to God for his redemption, his salvation, his promise-keeping, his forgiveness. It was about new light in place of darkness, new life in place of death, the coming of peace.

I sometimes feel so sad when people in church can't muster a prayer of gratitude or thanks when the opportunity is given. Too many are rendered speechless by their own reticence. We need to encourage one another by recognizing God's goodness to us, to his whole creation. Zechariah would never forget the day he met with God; he would never forget to be thankful for all that God had done in his history and the history of his people—and neither should we.

This Christmas, heavenly Father,
grant us your spirit of thankfulness.
As the cards arrive from friends and family,

we thank you for human relationships;
as we enjoy the festive fare,
we thank you for good food and all our material blessings;
as we sing the carols,
we thank you for the opportunity to praise you;
as we gaze at the baby in the manger,
we thank you that you keep your promises.
We give thanks, with a grateful heart. Amen.

23 December

ELIZABETH: LEAPING FOR JOY

At that time Mary got ready and hurried to a town in the hill country of Judea, where she entered Zechariah's home and greeted Elizabeth. When Elizabeth heard Mary's greeting, the baby leaped in her womb, and Elizabeth was filled with the Holy Spirit. In a loud voice she exclaimed: 'Blessed are you among women, and blessed is the child you will bear! But why am I so favoured, that the mother of my Lord should come to me? As soon as the sound of your greeting reached my ears, the baby in my womb leaped for joy. Blessed is she who has believed that what the Lord has said to her will be accomplished!'
LUKE 1:39–45

If Zechariah's life was changed by that day in the temple, then so was Elizabeth's!

Zechariah had headed off for Jerusalem for his twice-yearly stint of duty in the temple. We don't know whether he was able to get news to Elizabeth that the lot had fallen on him and his great moment was to come. We do know that he came home a few days later, speechless, facing the task of communicating to his wife exactly what had happened without using words. Maybe there was a lengthy session of charades (three syllables, proper name; first syllable, laughing, happy, jolly… GAY; second syllable, round, cow, milk, cheese, round cheese, French round cheese, camembert… BRIE; whole word, wings, high wings, angel… got it: GABRIEL!), or, more likely, calling for the writing tablet that he would need when family and friends challenged Elizabeth's assertion that their baby's name was to be John (Luke 1:63).

Even that little detail of the story is a reminder that then, as so often now, a woman can easily be snubbed or ignored, especially when there is a husband who is assumed to have the final word. We have no idea whether Elizabeth ever questioned the accepted order of things. Zechariah was the priest, he went to the temple and he had the deep religious experience. Even on a secular level, it is not unknown for the gap in daily experience to be a source of tension in a marriage relationship: husband has a big day at work; wife has to catch up with all the consequences. It is part of the potential for joy, support and mutuality—or frustration, incomprehension and tension.

Every married couple has to work through the way that experience gained in the absence of the other is shared when they are together again. I had the privilege of travelling to some of the most remote and exciting parts of the world during my 25 years with Tearfund: paddling dugout canoes deep in the rainforest; trekking on horseback into the Argentinian Chaco; flying towards the Mountains of the Moon in Uganda in a tiny plane while making a video with Cliff Richard. Susan had the privilege of staying at home, looking after the children, encouraging them after a trying day at school: as far as she was concerned, the main advantage of my overseas travel was that at least she had the use of the car while I was away! I came back, bursting with stories of the hard and wonderful experiences, wrestling over how they should be understood, assimilated and communicated; Susan would have the joys and frustrations of domestic life, as well as her work, to share—and a reminder for me of the jobs that were still waiting to be done.

Coming home was always enjoyable, always welcome, but we had to learn to make allowances for the space that the other needed to catch up and offload, choosing the time to share and the time to listen. One of the great joys of my life has been the opportunity, more recently, to travel together and share in those experiences directly. Peru was the one place I had visited that Susan was particularly keen to experience for herself, so it was great for us to be able to go together, for me to see the country as a tourist, and for Susan to glimpse a little of the life of the people who make the

Tearcraft goods that we had spent so much time selling in the 1970s.

Now the tables are turned. Susan is on the board of Release International, a charity supporting the persecuted church around the world, and she has become the one who travels, without me, to the challenging and evocative areas of our world: Iran, Nigeria and Sri Lanka. On the day she was leaving for Iran, our elder daughter overheard a friend at church asking how I would manage while Susan was away. Cue explosion! 'Mum had to manage while he jetted all round the world…' was the gist of her response.

Mind you, I feel I can empathize a little with Elizabeth. I know what it is like to be far away when something of enormous spiritual significance takes place for one's spouse: I was in Mexico City, phoning home from a call box on the street outside the hotel, when Susan told me about a very special experience of the Holy Spirit, which was an immediate blessing and significantly changed her life. There are times when being apart seems the greatest burden, and the longing to be together almost overwhelming. Every couple has to learn the rhythm of living together, rejoicing together, weeping together—especially when they have been apart and had very different experiences of life.

I am conscious, though, that I would find it very difficult to empathize with Elizabeth in, for her, the most significant impact of Zechariah's moment of blessing. Childlessness in our society can be an enormous tragedy for a woman who longs for the blessing of a child; Elizabeth lived at a time when it was seen not as a tragedy but a curse, a cause of shame—and a shame that was focused on the wife. The shame may also have been linked with concern for the future, as it is in so many societies today where poverty means that there is no state pension, and children are the only guarantee of security in old age. Elizabeth had lived with this reality for years, and now the biological clock had ticked away, leaving no hope.

What a turnaround! This story bubbles with the joy and delight that Elizabeth exudes as she discovers that there is to be a blessing for her, for them both together, as a result of Zechariah's blessing. She is to have a child. Moreover, this child will have a significant role to play in God's plan of salvation. And the angel promises Zechariah what every parent would long to hear: that the child will be a joy and delight, filled with the Holy Spirit from his birth.

So it is two excited women who meet up to compare notes, one old, the other young—sharing the joy of expectancy, recognizing their role in God's purposes and understanding something of the significance of the babies they bear. The babies themselves find the joy infectious, it seems. Every mother knows the moment when the kicking of the unborn infant is not a discomfort but a glorious affirmation of life. Elizabeth was convinced that her child had recognized Jesus, even while both were in their mothers' wombs.

Some people see this passage as biblical evidence that unborn babies are sentient beings, capable of life and deserving of protection. You do not have to be a militant pro-life activist to be profoundly uneasy about the ease with which unwanted babies have become a throwaway item in today's society. Some mothers choose a termination of pregnancy with careful thought and heavy hearts; some treat it as an acceptable method of eliminating a problem with a minimum of fuss. I suspect that those who have longed most for a child feel the most sadness about the thousands of unborn children every year who are denied the opportunity even of making a start on life.

Elizabeth was promised a baby when all hope has gone, but not everyone is promised a miracle, however much we may want or need one—except for the miracle of the new birth. God has promised eternal life to those who believe in his Son, and in that respect each one of us can enter into the blessing pronounced by Elizabeth to Mary: 'Blessed is she who has believed that what the Lord has said to her will be accomplished!' God has not only offered you the gift of forgiveness and salvation; he longs for you to receive that gift, to know it and be assured of it. Don't be one of those who can never be convinced that God really means what he says.

This study has touched on some of the deep areas of life: marriage, childlessness, abortion. My prayer is that the Holy Spirit will have given sensitivity in your reading wherever it is needed. I am all too aware of the ease with which offence can be given when none is intended. Even in church, people can discover the uncanny ability of human beings to say nothing when a word of sympathy and encouragement is desperately needed, and to say something crass when silence would have been golden. Not everyone's sorrow is turned to joy as it was for Elizabeth. Part of the very deepest Christian maturity is to rejoice at the blessing of others when we are longing for blessing ourselves.

Dear God, your word says 'As a mother comforts her child,
so will I comfort you.'
Please comfort those today who need your comfort:
those who long for children;
those who long for their children.
Grant us sensitivity to weep with those who weep
and rejoice with those who rejoice,
so that we give your value to women.
Give us the right words when words are needed,
and silence when they are not.
Help us to encourage those for whom
this time of year is especially painful.
Help us to share in the joy of those
who enjoy every minute of it.
For Jesus' sake. Amen.

24 December

JOHN THE BAPTIST: PREPARE THE WAY

The beginning of the gospel about Jesus Christ, the Son of God. It is written in Isaiah the prophet: 'I will send my messenger ahead of you, who will prepare your way—a voice of one calling in the desert, "Prepare the way for the Lord, make straight paths for him."' And so John came, baptizing in the desert region and preaching a baptism of repentance for the forgiveness of sins. The whole Judean countryside and all the people of Jerusalem went out to him. Confessing their sins, they were baptized by him in the Jordan River. John wore clothing made of camel's hair, with a leather belt round his waist, and he ate locusts and wild honey. And this was his message: 'After me will come one more powerful than I, the thongs of whose sandals I am not worthy to stoop down and untie. I baptize you with water, but he will baptize you with the Holy Spirit.' At that time Jesus came from Nazareth in Galilee and was baptized by John in the Jordan.

MARK 1:1–9

Christmas Eve! It is a day of preparation, full of expectation of the glorious day that is to follow. In reality, it is often a day of panic, when the shops will close on the possibility of getting that last present (just the thing that they always wanted) and that last vital ingredient of the Christmas dinner. Every year you promise yourself that you will be better organized and give yourself more time to enjoy the anticipation of Christmas. My wife and I have always enjoyed the Christmas Eve midnight communion—a simple moment of peace and fellowship, rejoicing in the sign of God's love represented in bread and wine, and represented in a baby born to make it possible for us to have communion with God.

If you have managed to find time, on this day of all days, to open the pages of this book, you have come to spend time with the one who is the patron saint of preparation, the one who appeared by the side of a river in the desert, calling out, 'Prepare the way for the Lord.' I always feel some element of identification with John. It's not just that he was called 'the Baptist' and I have worshipped in Baptist churches for the past 35 years. I don't think it's because I always think of him as a bearded, unkempt hippy figure from the 1960s: I have been bearded, occasionally unkempt, but never really a hippy. And while I will confess to a leather belt, I have certainly not gone in for wearing camel–hair coats or a diet of locusts and wild honey.

I suspect the truth is that I have a sneaking regard for the prophetic outsider, the one who stands and rails against the religious establishment of his time, the angry young man of the first century. I am not too good with certainty, especially the certainty of others. That makes me an awkward member of a group, always wishing things were different, always asking awkward questions, always challenging authority (although, unlike Jesus in Matthew 3:7, I have never called anyone 'a brood of vipers'). I was a deacon as a young man at the Baptist church where Susan and I were married. Some years later, after we had moved away, I was invited back to preach. Afterwards, one of my former fellow deacons commented that he didn't think I was as angry as I had been when he had known me on the diaconate. He thought he was paying me a compliment; I was quite disturbed, convinced I must be abandoning my principles and settling into middle-class and middle-aged conformity.

John the Baptist is part of the Christmas story. Six months older than his cousin, he recognized Jesus in his mother's womb, and announced him to the world as 'the Lamb of God, who takes away the sin of the world' (John 1:29), just as the angels had explained his mission 30 years earlier. He is a link between the first blaze of glory and the emergence of Jesus into public ministry. He consciously echoes the Old Testament prophets and hands on the baton to the promised Messiah. He knows that the birth of Jesus is the dawn of a new age; as Jesus strides towards him by the Jordan, he knows that each step is a step closer to the coming kingdom.

On Christmas Eve, as we get ready for Christmas Day, it's worth reflecting on exactly how John prepared the world for Jesus. First, we are told that he baptized, 'preaching a baptism of repentance for the forgiveness of sins'. You will forgive me, I trust, if as a Baptist preacher I indulge my identification with this verse. I have preached for the whole of my adult life, ever since my father encouraged me in the open-air meetings that he used to help to organize in the parks of Birmingham. It was a curious experience: sometimes we would use a splendid Edwardian bandstand, sometimes just a corner of the park, but often I would not be aware that anyone was listening, which was quite useful for a nervous beginner in his mid-teens. I'm grateful that I had the opportunity to make a start; I can't help wondering whether John practised in the desert, with only the occasional bird as a listener.

It's only more recently that I have had the opportunity to preach and baptize. It's a wonderful privilege to share in this act of witness with people whom you have known a little and watched begin or restart their journey of faith. It's a privilege to have the opportunity, especially if they have brought friends and family who have never witnessed a service of baptism before, to explain what it is all about. Even when we use the local swimming pool, and the service is part of an evening that includes swimming, eating and worship as well as the baptism, we still make the same serious point that John made two thousand years ago: baptism is all about a decision to turn away from sin and receive the gift of forgiveness from God. The New Testament emphasizes the symbolism of the ceremony: the washing clean from the dirt of sin, the dying to the old life and being raised to a new life. There's further symbolism: once the decision is made, you place yourself in the hands of others to carry out the baptism; once we make the decision to repent and turn to God, we have to trust him, to be able to receive forgiveness. We can no more baptize ourselves than we can forgive our own sin—and that's true whichever tradition of baptism we are most comfortable with.

John was aware of the limitations of his baptism. It could not take away sin, but he was preparing the way for the one who could. Jesus' baptism would be more than symbolic: he would baptize with the Holy Spirit, the giver of life. The Christian is born again of the Spirit and baptized with the Spirit—new life, new lifestyle.

John did not simply urge repentance; he knew that lasting change was needed. 'Produce fruit in keeping with repentance,' he urged (Luke 3:8), and he spelled out what this meant: generosity to those in need, the rejection of greed. In this too he was preparing the way for Jesus, who would not only take up his message, but, by bequeathing the presence of his Spirit, would make possible the reality of the fruit of the Spirit.

John was a relative of Jesus, but he acknowledged that he was in a different league. John was not even worthy to perform the menial task of a servant. Yet Jesus affirmed that 'no one ever born on this earth is greater than John the Baptist. But whoever is least in the kingdom of heaven is greater than John' (Matthew 11:11, CEV). Nothing illustrates better the difference made by the first Advent. John prepared the way; Jesus is the way.

Dear God, as we prepare to celebrate the birth of your son, allow us the privilege of preparing the way for Jesus in the lives of others. Amen.

25 December

MARY: THE MOTHER AT THE MANGER

So Joseph also went up from the town of Nazareth in Galilee to Judea, to Bethlehem the town of David, because he belonged to the house and line of David. He went there to register with Mary, who was pledged to be married to him and was expecting a child. While they were there, the time came for the baby to be born, and she gave birth to her firstborn, a son. She wrapped him in cloths and placed him in a manger, because there was no room for them in the inn.
LUKE 2:4–7

Happy Christmas!

When families get together on birthdays, as long as parents are around, there will be a tendency to reminisce about the moment of birth. Our two children have heard the stories countless times. Katharine was born in the middle of one of the hottest summers on record—and that's my defence to the charge of being a wimp. After a labour lasting two days, I managed to miss the vital two minutes because I thought I was going to faint. With Helen, it was a different story. This time I was rushed out of the delivery room just after the birth as Susan was haemorrhaging and there was urgent medical attention to be given. It was two hours before I was told that mother and baby were doing fine. But these are the details that stay within the family: what matters most is that the babies born have grown up and made their own impact on the world.

There are no gory details in this simple account—not that one would want them. It's just that the sanitized Christmas card pictures of stables and mangers can obscure the fact that this was a real birth in difficult circumstances, preceded by a lengthy journey, almost certainly on foot, with Mary close to giving birth. It took place in a room shared with animals (probably the downstairs area or the courtyard of the house), a room unlikely to have had fresh straw provided, and animals determined to make sure it didn't stay fresh in any case. The moment of birth is the single most dangerous time in anyone's life: risk analysis consultants might well conclude that focusing the whole success of a several-thousand-year plan on the safe birth of one child was a high-risk strategy.

Every time I think of the Christmas nativity scene, my mind goes back to two experiences in my travels with Tearfund. One was in Ethiopia in 1984, at the height of the great famine. It was the first time I entered a *tukul*, a traditional rural home. It was a small round hut, no more than about seven or eight metres in diameter. We entered out of the blazing midday heat into almost complete darkness, and as my eyes got used to the light filtering in through the narrow entrance I realized that a few sheep and goats had been brought into the home, out of the sun. They would have been there during the night as well. I took a photograph, the flash blazing in the darkness. I had no idea what I had pointed the camera at, so it was only when the photo came back from the developers that I discovered there had been a tiny baby asleep in the corner.

A few years earlier, in India, I was visiting a village which, I was told, had been inhabited for six thousand years. As we rounded a corner in the path, we glimpsed a house, with a young woman aged no more than 15 sitting outside, tenderly gazing down at the tiny baby that suckled at her breast, and ignoring the cow that was contentedly chewing the cud just a few feet away. It was a timeless scene, a reminder that the Christmas story is not so far removed from the common experience of millions of the world's inhabitants. This is one reason why I think that even on Christmas Day it is worth noting that infant and maternal mortality are among the most significant symptoms of poverty in our world: in one African country, one in ten of all women die in childbirth.

I have some yellowing Mother's Day sermon notes that date back to 1977, written for a little Baptist chapel in South London. I felt then that it was a little daring to take Mary as the topic, given all the debate and division generated over the centuries by consideration of her role and status within the church. Yet it is a great pity if, because of our particular tradition, we miss some of the beautifully simple lessons to be learnt from a young girl chosen by God for an awesome task.

The message from the angel Gabriel was disturbing, shocking. Her whole life was to be turned upside down, her reputation called into question, her fiancé's trust in her stretched to breaking point. But she had a willingness to accept God's will, to embrace the new horizon opened up to her. Her final words to the angel show us how to accept God's will for our lives: 'I am the Lord's servant. May it be to me as you have said' (Luke 1:38).

'Jesus is for life, not just for Christmas,' says at least one church noticeboard. Every mother knows that the tiny baby who brings so much joy is a commitment for life. If you look at the nativity set or the scene on the Christmas card, have you ever wondered what Mary is doing? The Bible says that she was thinking: when she heard the shepherds' story, she 'pondered': 'Mary kept thinking about all this and wondering what it meant' (Luke 2:19, CEV). After discovering Jesus in the temple as a young man, confounding the scholars, she 'kept on thinking about all that had happened' (Luke 2:51, CEV). If you have found time to think about Jesus and the meaning of Christmas today, and over this Advent period, that's great. Keep doing it! The more we engage our minds and our spirits with the reality of Jesus, the more he will be able to share his life with us.

Mary's 30 years of thinking and pondering lay behind her willingness to back her son at a vital moment. The local wedding in Cana was in danger of becoming a horrible embarrassment for the father of the bride. Instantly Mary communicates to the servants the attitude she had shown to the angel Gabriel: 'Do whatever Jesus tells you to do' (John 2:5, CEV). At this point Jesus had performed no miracles: Mary was a woman of faith—and water was turned into wine, gallons of it.

Mary was also a woman who knew how to praise God. When she meets Elizabeth, who confirms to her the significance of her baby, she bursts into song:

My soul glorifies the Lord
and my spirit rejoices in God my Saviour,
for he has been mindful
of the humble state of his servant.
From now on all generations will call me blessed,
for the Mighty One has done great things for me—
holy is his name.
His mercy extends to those who fear him,
from generation to generation.
He has performed mighty deeds with his arm;
he has scattered those who are proud in their inmost thoughts.
He has brought down rulers from their thrones
but has lifted up the humble.
He has filled the hungry with good things
but has sent the rich away empty.
He has helped his servant Israel,
remembering to be merciful
to Abraham and his descendants forever,
even as he said to our fathers.

LUKE 1:46–55

Mary rejoices in a God who is for the humble and the poor; she exults in a God who does great things for his people; she acknowledges with joy that this is a God who keeps his promises. Mary knew that God was working in human history and she rejoiced that she had a part to play. In that she was no different from you and me—so you have every right to stand in the group around the manger, and, on Christmas Day of all days, it's worth giving yourself time to ponder.

What Child is this who, laid to rest
On Mary's lap is sleeping?
Whom Angels greet with anthems sweet,
While shepherds watch are keeping?

This, this is Christ the King,
Whom shepherds guard and Angels sing;
Haste, haste, to bring Him praise,
The Babe, the Son of Mary.

WILLIAM CHATTERTON DIX (1837–98)

JOSEPH: BEST SUPPORTING ACTOR

This is how the birth of Jesus Christ came about: His mother Mary was pledged to be married to Joseph, but before they came together, she was found to be with child through the Holy Spirit. Because Joseph her husband was a righteous man and did not want to expose her to public disgrace, he had in mind to divorce her quietly. But after he had considered this, an angel of the Lord appeared to him in a dream and said, 'Joseph son of David, do not be afraid to take Mary home as your wife, because what is conceived in her is from the Holy Spirit. She will give birth to a son, and you are to give him the name Jesus, because he will save his people from their sins.'

All this took place to fulfil what the Lord had said through the prophet: 'The virgin will be with child and will give birth to a son, and they will call him Immanuel'—which means, 'God with us'. When Joseph woke up, he did what the angel of the Lord had commanded him and took Mary home as his wife. But he had no union with her until she gave birth to a son. And he gave him the name Jesus.

MATTHEW 1:18–25

I think Joseph is the unsung hero of the Christmas story. Almost everything we know about him is as a result of his life being turned upside down almost by proxy. Mary is chosen to be the mother of Jesus… there must have been a moment when Joseph reflected that he might have been consulted. His life and expectations were thrown into turmoil. One minute, he is an engaged man, looking forward to his wedding. The next, he is being asked to accept that his bride-to-be is pregnant, not as the result of infidelity or a moment of illicit passion, but as a result of God's direct intervention.

Suddenly he has to make deeply significant decisions at great speed. First, in the midst of his shock and disappointment, he is still able to be protective of Mary, concerned at least to end the relationship quietly and to spare her as much public disgrace as possible. The practice of engagement here was very different from modern Britain's—although, once again, more recognizable to many from the developing world. Parents made the wedding matches for their children; thus, children could be engaged as young as three or four years old. The actual wedding could take place not long after the young girl had reached puberty. A year before the marriage was to take place, however, engagement became betrothal—a binding commitment to each other that could be ended only by both parties signing a bill of divorce, even though the marriage had been neither celebrated nor consummated. If the groom died during this betrothal period, the woman was regarded as a widowed virgin.

Of course, there has been much controversy about the biblical insistence that Jesus was born of a virgin. Some people argue that the story was made up in the later years of the first century, when the Gospels were written, to boost the status of Jesus and to claim fulfilment of an Old Testament prophecy: 'a virgin shall conceive' (Isaiah 7:14, KJV). Further, it is said that the claim was based on a false translation of this verse, because the Hebrew word used can also mean simply 'young woman'. I do wonder if the choice of word is just a recognition of the assumption that young women would be unmarried and therefore virgins: when they were married they would no longer be regarded as young women. Certainly, when 70 Jewish scholars translated Isaiah from Hebrew into Greek in 200BC, they chose the Greek word that could only mean 'virgin'—and they could not have been making things up to accommodate the story of Jesus.

There is a theologically important reason why Jesus' conception should be a miracle of this kind (although the sceptics see this as a further reason why the story would have been concocted by the Gospel writers). If the tendency to sin was inherent in every human descendant of Adam and Eve, then somehow the line of inheritance of this spiritual DNA had to be broken if the Son of God was to be fully human and fully divine. And if Jesus was—and is—fully human and fully divine, this is, to my mind, an even greater miracle than the virgin birth itself. After all, if the Holy Spirit was responsible for the creation of the entire universe, to conceive a tiny baby was a relatively simple task.

Faced with the awful, but unlikely, possibility that Mary had somehow betrayed his trust, Joseph was sufficiently convinced by the angel to change his mind and, instead of divorcing her, to embark on the harder path of standing by Mary, taking her as his wife and, in effect, publicly sharing her disgrace. How difficult that would have been for one who is described as 'a righteous man'—or, as the CEV footnote puts it, 'a man who always did the right thing' (Matthew 1:19). There are moments for all of us when doing the right thing may actually mean losing our reputation for doing the right thing. Those are the moments when we have to be concerned about God's opinion, not that of our friends and neighbours. It is fascinating—and sometimes tragic—that many people outside the church have a sharper view of this reality than those inside. The attempt to cover up wrongdoing to preserve reputation can be the quickest way to lose that reputation.

So Joseph did the right thing. Perhaps he was doing the right thing by taking Mary with him to Bethlehem: she had no need to travel, but maybe he preferred to be with her than to leave her behind, to give birth surrounded by whispers and pointing fingers. And Joseph did the right thing in naming the baby. Jesus is the Greek form of Joshua, which means 'God's salvation' and was a common name among the Jewish people. For some, it echoed the great hero Joshua, who had brought the people into the promised land; for others, it was an expression of hope that their son would do the same for a new generation, and become the salvation of Israel.

Joseph is by far the least acknowledged member of the holy family, for obvious reasons. But he has been given an interesting niche in the life and traditions of some parts of the Christian Church. Pope

Pius IX proclaimed him the patron of the Universal Church in December 1870, and, slightly more quirkily, I gather that he is also the patron saint against doubt and hesitation, as well as the patron saint of fighting communism, and of a happy death. Even more amazingly, he is apparently key to finding a good buyer and a good price if you are selling your home—but you have to bury a small statue of Joseph upside down next to your 'For Sale' sign, while saying an appropriate prayer.

Joseph's life was turned inside out by a baby. The assumption is that he was much older than Mary. We know he was a carpenter, and we know that his last appearance in the story was when Jesus was 12 and visited Jerusalem for the first time. How difficult did he find it when Jesus said that he was in the temple because he had to be 'about his father's business' (Luke 2:49, KJV)? Joseph was the father who wasn't a father; but he was the man who did the right thing.

Loving God, heavenly Father,
our world needs men who are concerned to do the right thing,
fathers who protect and support their wives
and care for their children.
We pray for a renewed vision of godly masculinity
that will inspire men to walk with you. Amen.

27 December

SIMEON: A DIVINE APPOINTMENT

Now there was a man in Jerusalem called Simeon, who was righteous and devout. He was waiting for the consolation of Israel, and the Holy Spirit was upon him. It had been revealed to him by the Holy Spirit that he would not die before he had seen the Lord's Christ. Moved by the Spirit, he went into the temple courts. When the parents brought in the child Jesus to do for him what the custom of the Law required, Simeon took him in his arms and praised God, saying: 'Sovereign Lord, as you have promised, you now dismiss your servant in peace. For my eyes have seen your salvation, which you have prepared in the sight of all people, a light for revelation to the Gentiles and for glory to your people Israel.'

The child's father and mother marvelled at what was said about him. Then Simeon blessed them and said to Mary, his mother: 'This child is destined to cause the falling and rising of many in Israel, and to be a sign that will be spoken against, so that the thoughts of many hearts will be revealed. And a sword will pierce your own soul too.'

LUKE 2:25–35

Simeon was not the only one who had been waiting, but he was the one whose hope and patience were rewarded by this special encounter. Something he had longed for through his whole life came about in his old age. I recall one of the first times that Susan and I offered hospitality to a real-live good old-fashioned missionary. She had gone to the Ivory Coast along with her husband in the 1930s; she had begun the whole process of Bible translation from scratch, writing down a previously unwritten language. She had protected her papers from forest fires, praying as the flames advanced, and watching as the wind veered away at the last moment. Forty years later, she had retired, presented with the first printed copy of the New Testament in that language. It is a rare blessing, and one to be cherished, to end one's days with a deep sense of fulfilment. We would all love to be 'dismissed' with a deep sense of God's peace, and enter the presence of God, where there is peace for evermore.

Simeon demonstrates a wonderful life balance. He was righteous and devout. We've already met the 'righteous' word: it's the one applied to Joseph. It has an expanded meaning: someone whose way of thinking, feeling and acting is entirely in line with the will of God. 'Devout' suggests someone religious, ready and willing to observe corporate worship and private devotions. I get the feeling that Simeon loved to be in the temple. In my experience, it is all too easy to get out of balance. Some Christians are so busy with church, prayer meetings and quiet times that they have no time for people, for building relationships, for working out their faith in the crucible of everyday life. Others are activists, uneasy with quiet and reflection, readily bored with religious observance. Jesus spent time alone with his heavenly father, and was fully engaged in meeting the needs of the people. It's the resources we gain in the Spirit that provide us with something to give to those we meet in the activity of life.

Simeon was waiting for the 'consolation of Israel'. No one doubts that this is a reference to the expected and anticipated Messiah, but it is an interesting phrase. 'Consolation' carries the sense of comfort: indeed, this is the same root as the word used about the Holy Spirit, who will be the promised 'comforter' (John 14:16, KJV). It has that sense of offering sympathy and encouragement to the one who has been beaten down by life. But there is something more, and the clue is in the make-up of the words.

'Comfort' comes from two Latin words meaning 'with' and 'strength' (*forte*). There is a lovely section of the Bayeux tapestry which is captioned 'William comforts his troops'. And there he is, comforting away—by prodding them with a spear! He is giving them strength, even encouraging them, filling them with new courage at the point of the spear. Encouragement can give you the strength to keep going. Every Christian has been promised the Spirit to comfort them—but his comforting is designed to give you the strength to continue. Barnabas is described as the 'son of consolation' (Acts 4:36, KJV), or, as the CEV puts it, 'one who encourages others'. It's a great gift to have; it's one of the ways we are all strengthened for the journey.

I recall the first time I spoke to a well-known Christian leader and preacher. He had been preaching at the time of the Falklands conflict between Britain and Argentina, and he had emphasized that Christians in these two warring countries were citizens of the same kingdom, and therefore had far more things in common than things that separated them. I happened to bump into him afterwards, and told him I thought this had been a most helpful point to make. To my surprise, he reacted really positively, and was clearly grateful that I had spoken to him. Years later, I got to know him quite well, and I reminded him of this incident and of my surprise that he had been so interested in what I, a stranger, had had to say. 'Surely you know, every preacher needs to be told they have done well,' he replied. 'They are desperate for reassurance.' I think he's right. It's worth remembering as you approach the door of the church on a Sunday!

Simeon must have been bursting with encouragement that day in the temple. The moment for which he had longed had arrived. Mary and Joseph had come to observe the law concerning purification after childbirth (Leviticus 12:2–8), and to dedicate their firstborn to the service of God. Simeon recognizes the baby as the one who will fulfil the law and serve God's purposes in all their entirety, and bursts out in his song of joy and praise, often known as the Nunc Dimittis from the opening words, 'Now dismiss…'. The song reveals that Simeon was steeped in the Old Testament word of God. Of course he was: he was searching for the signs of God's intervention in human history.

Simeon's eyes had seen the salvation prepared in the sight of all people: as the prophet had said, 'all the ends of the earth will see the salvation of our God' (Isaiah 52:10). Simeon rejoiced at the realization that the consolation of Israel was God's gift for the whole world, for all the nations. 'Declare his glory among the nations' (Psalm 96:3) must have rung out around the temple on many occasions. And finally, Simeon refers to one of the great promises relating to the coming of the Messiah: 'I, the Lord, have called you in righteousness; I will take hold of your hand. I will keep you and will make you to be a covenant for the people and a light for the Gentiles, to open eyes that are blind, to free captives from prison and to release from the dungeon those who sit in darkness' (Isaiah 42:6–7).

Simeon finishes with a bleak word of reality for Mary. The mixture of joy and sadness that is the lot of every mother, of everyone who dares to love, would be just as true for her. One of the most haunting images of Mel Gibson's film *The Passion of the Christ* is the face of Mary as she watches her son being tortured and killed. As Graham Kendrick's song puts it so poignantly:

And did she see there
In the straw by his head a thorn?
And did she smell myrrh
In the air on that starry night?

GRAHAM KENDRICK © 1994 MAKE WAY MUSIC

Jesus was the consolation of Israel; but he would be 'a sign that will be spoken against'. Simeon knew that the Christmas journey led outside the city to a place of pain and suffering. He rejoiced; he could depart in peace; but he knew that peace came at a price.

God of young and old alike, thank you so much for all the encouragement we have received, especially from those who are old in years but mature in their faith. As we get older, give us expectation, hope, and the ability to encourage others with grace and humility. Through Jesus Christ our Lord. Amen.

28 December

ANNA: WORSHIP AND WITNESS

There was also a prophetess, Anna, the daughter of Phanuel, of the tribe of Asher. She was very old; she had lived with her husband seven years after her marriage, and then was a widow until she was eighty-four. She never left the temple but worshipped night and day, fasting and praying. Coming up to them at that very moment, she gave thanks to God and spoke about the child to all who were looking forward to the redemption of Jerusalem.

LUKE 2:36–38

I think I would like to have met Anna. These few verses summon up for me a picture of a woman of deep devotion, with twinkling eyes, full of life and energy. She had clearly known sadness: the implication of these verses is that she had known a long period of widowhood after a very short marriage. The tradition is that she was married at 14, so she might have known 63 years of singleness. But she had opted to use her time developing her relationship with God, spending every waking moment in praise, prayer and fasting.

To many in our secularized society, this would sound like madness; to many in our churches, it would sound like dangerous fanaticism! I am an activist by nature; I would struggle to live like this. I have also learned, however, that just as Simeon reminds us that we all need a healthy balance between devotion and action in our lives, Anna is a reminder that the church needs a balance too. A church with all activists and no contemplatives can lack spiritual depth, insight and stability. A church with all contemplatives and no activists can become inward-looking and self-serving. This is exactly why Paul likened the church to a body, made up of different parts but all needing each other to function properly (1 Corinthians 12).

As I have grown older, I have realized just how much the church relies on women like Anna. Her name (the Hebrew version is Hannah) means 'gracious'. There is an unsung army of gracious women who give their devotion to God and their time to the church. They are often ignored or patronized when they should be supported and encouraged. I am grateful for some in the church where I grew up who, so I discovered, had faithfully prayed for me every day long after I had left and moved away. When I was a boy they were, I confess, no more than old women. Now I have a grown up a little, I know that some were mighty warriors of God.

It has been a real blessing to be married to a woman who has given time to her walk with God. I know she has appreciated the fact that, not needing to work, she has had the time to give to others, and time to spend in prayer and fasting, receiving from God so that she has resources to share with others. What a tragedy that godliness has become such an unfashionable quality, even within the church! What a tragedy that godliness is equated with dourness and lifelessness! I am so grateful that God has allowed me to share my life with someone vivacious, sparkling, passionate—and godly.

Every woman will have noticed that the Christmas story is a wonderful affirmation of women, and I don't think that is because there is a baby at the centre! The Gospels as a whole are full of stories of women who supported Jesus, whose lives were changed by him, who formed deep relationships with him. It is appalling and tragic that so many women now experience the church as a place where their contribution is discounted, their views marginalized, their perspective undervalued. Most of the time, this is not the result of a conscious policy; it just happens—but it shouldn't. Church leaders need to make a special effort in gender awareness. This is nothing to do with political correctness, or even theological discussions about the ordination of women. It is simply about valuing people as God values them, living our lives on the basis of God's values as revealed in the Bible. Anna was an old woman in a society where men thanked God that they had not been born women; she worshipped in the temple, which had areas that women were not allowed to enter—but she was able to hold the baby born to be the saviour of the world.

That was the basis for her worship: she praised God. It was also the basis for her witness: she spoke to people about Jesus. Anna can teach us something about what it means to share our faith. I will try to avoid gender-stereotyping myself here, but Anna was a natural talker, and a natural talker about Jesus. It so happens that most of the people I have met who have been like this have been women. They definitely have a gift: they don't need to manipulate the conversation to talk about Jesus; it just happens. They can never understand why it doesn't happen to others, because it is so natural for them that they assume it is the same for everyone.

With Anna, too, there was consistency of behaviour. The authenticity of her conversation came from her obvious commitment and enthusiasm. Nothing destroys the witness of the church more than words not backed by action, or actions that belie the words. In the 21st century, I do not believe that the church in Britain is declining because we haven't yet discovered the right evangelistic programme. It's because not enough of us have lived for Jesus and talked about Jesus with enthusiasm and commitment. It's because we've been convinced that faith-sharing is about getting people into church and then persuading them to believe—when we really need to get the church out among the people, living such lives of loving sacrifice for and in our communities that people are persuaded that they want to know about our beliefs.

The Alpha course has had a real impact. It focuses on explaining the truth about Jesus to those who want to hear. And I know that while some come out of genuine curiosity to explore Christianity, far more come because they have a friendship with someone who invites them, someone whose life and conversation have made them think that there might be more to religion than they assumed. Our church was thrilled when a group of young people on a local estate indicated that they wanted to make a commitment to following Jesus. It came after an investment of time and energy under the 'Soul in the City' banner—two major efforts of community involvement during the summer holidays sandwiching a year of weekly evenings playing football and chatting.

I worked at Tearfund for 25 years. My biggest concern was to help Christians to realize that relief and development work was not an alternative to what had been traditionally understood as evangelism; it was an essential part of evangelism. The Bible is clear that telling people about the love of God is sensible only when it is also demonstrated in action. If I want my children to grow up to share my beliefs, the one way I can guarantee failure is to do nothing other than preach to them. But if I really love them, then I will be concerned about their bodies and their minds as well as their spirits. They will be fed, clothed and cared for, given time and encouragement. I will want the best for them in every way, because that is what love is like. I will want them to be able to choose to follow Jesus for themselves, not to be coerced or manipulated into it.

It would be tragic to dismiss Anna as no more than an old woman who got to hold a baby. She was a woman who dedicated her life to God, who met with Jesus and loved to tell people about him. She showed integrity, enthusiasm and commitment. I would love to know a few more Annas.

God of goodness, God of hope,
send your Spirit so that we can live lives that honour your name.
Send your Spirit so that we can commend your name
with words of integrity and warmth.
Send your Spirit to breathe renewed passion for Jesus
into tired lives. For Jesus' sake. Amen.

29 DECEMBER–4 JANUARY

A SENSE OF PURPOSE

INTRODUCTION

So a baby is born: Emmanuel, God with us. This is the great miracle of Christmas—the promise made at the beginning of time, made good when the time was right. But the Christmas story is not complete in itself. Thirty years later, the baby has grown into a man, who bursts into national prominence from the moment that he is baptized by John and affirmed by Father and Holy Spirit.

From that moment on, Jesus' life is one of response to the prompting of the Spirit as he follows a divine timetable for his life and ministry. The Gospels are rich in their insistence that at no time is Jesus the victim of circumstance or controlled by events. Each Gospel writer highlights his own perspective on God's great gift to his world, but they are united in revealing the Son of Man who is the Son of God and is entirely clear about his purpose in life—fulfilling prophecy, fulfilling the will of his Father, and fulfilling the divine appointments in the diary of salvation.

The time has come, the time was fulfilled, the time is at hand, the time is coming: these are the phrases of the Gospels that indicate the driving purpose of Jesus' life. So often, our lives are driven by time. To Jesus, though, time was a servant, not a master—a servant that provided the setting for Jesus to live a life of loving service as he moved towards the moment of sacrifice. His life is a pattern for us to follow; his death makes it possible for us to be forgiven and enter his kingdom; his resurrection and ascension are the forerunners to the gift of his Spirit, who inspires and equips us to live lives of worship as we play our part in God's purposes.

From heaven you came, helpless babe,
Entered our world, your glory veiled;
Not to be served but to serve,
And give Your life that we might live.

This is our God, the servant king,
He calls us now to follow him,
To bring our lives as a daily offering
Of worship to the servant king.

FROM 'THE SERVANT KING' BY GRAHAM KENDRICK

29 December

THE TIME HAS COME!

As Jesus was coming up out of the water, he saw heaven being torn open and the Spirit descending on him like a dove. And a voice came from heaven: 'You are my Son, whom I love; with you I am well pleased.' At once the Spirit sent him out into the desert, and he was in the desert for forty days, being tempted by Satan. He was with the wild animals, and angels attended him.

After John was put in prison, Jesus went into Galilee, proclaiming the good news of God. 'The time has come,' he said. 'The kingdom of God is near. Repent and believe the good news!' As Jesus walked beside the Sea of Galilee, he saw Simon and his brother Andrew casting a net into the lake, for they were fishermen. 'Come, follow me,' Jesus said, 'and I will make you fishers of men and women.' At once they left their nets and followed him. When he had gone a little farther, he saw James son of Zebedee and his brother John in a boat, preparing their nets. Without delay he called them, and they left their father Zebedee in the boat with the hired men and followed him.

They went to Capernaum, and when the Sabbath came, Jesus went into the synagogue and began to teach. The people were amazed at his teaching, because he taught them as one who had authority, not as the teachers of the law. Just then a man in their synagogue who was possessed by an evil spirit cried out, 'What do you want with us, Jesus of Nazareth? Have you come to destroy us? I know who you are—the Holy One of God!' 'Be quiet!' said Jesus sternly. 'Come out of him!'

MARK 1:10–25

Procrastination is the thief of time—not least because it's such a long word to write. But then, my besetting sin is all too often the tendency to work on the principle of 'why do today what I could think about putting off until tomorrow?' Mark's Gospel is the exact opposite: it is the Gospel of urgency. Significant episodes are described in brief. Nearly every one is linked to the next with a word like the snapping of fingers: 'then', 'at once', 'immediately', 'without delay'. Jesus is constantly on the move, walking here, going there; there is a buzz of energy in the writing that reflects the energy he was putting into his ministry.

Jesus arrives at the Jordan to be baptized by John. It is a highly charged moment, as Jesus is identified both as the 'Lamb of God' and as one so important that John is not even worthy to be his servant. But then he submits to John's baptism even though he has no need to, as far as forgiveness of sins is concerned, and a voice from heaven immediately announces that he is God's beloved Son. You or I would have wanted to take time to enjoy the moment, to chat to John, to talk to the crowd. Jesus, however, is immediately removed from this setting, away from the astonished crowds, and spends 40 days in the desert in a private battle with Satan.

Then he strides back into the area where he has grown up. He has been away for several weeks. John has been arrested; it is time to pick up the baton and pursue his ministry. The time has come! Jesus is walking by the lake, on the move. He sees two fishermen. He immediately offers them a new career. Simon and Andrew drop everything and accept. It's all over in minutes. Then there are two more fishermen. Jesus makes an instant decision, makes the offer, and they instantly accept. There's not much measured reflection going on here, no lengthy interview process subject to references, no instruction to go away and pray about it. There are times when it has to be now, not later.

One of those times is when we hear God demanding our full commitment. Most of us are highly skilled in finding good reasons to postpone that kind of decision. What's the danger in putting it off? One is that we miss the moment altogether, and it never returns—or, if it does, we realize just how much time we have wasted. My grandfather became a Christian in his 60s, and for the next 30 years never tired of saying how much he regretted having waited that long. It is not just about an initial decision; it's about making the most of the life that God has given to us. Every day we put off committing ourselves to God is a day that we miss out on being part of God's purposes, of seeing those glimpses of the kingdom that reveal all that's good about the good news. Jesus' offer of alternative employment did not come with tempting terms and conditions; it came with a promise of doing something of deep and eternal significance. People sometimes ask the question, 'What gets you out of bed in the morning?' There can be no better answer than 'to be part of what God is doing'.

There are moments in all our lives when we sense that the time has come. I remember a Saturday in my room at university when I knew that I wanted to spend the rest of my life with Susan. (One of the lecturers assured me that I was the only student he had ever known to finish three years at university with the same girlfriend as when he started. In fact, I was quite surprised she accepted my invitation to visit in my first term—but I'm glad she did!) Then, ten years later, we sat together in the car, parked by the Thames, working out the implications of leaving my teaching job and accepting a position with Tearfund—and once again, I knew that the time had come to make the commitment for a new phase of life.

Jesus had gone into the desert to prepare for this moment. John was no longer able to proclaim his message. This was the time (*kairos*), which was, in the literal meaning of the Greek, 'fulfilled', just as the Gospel writers record that a prophecy had been fulfilled. It was as if time was being measured by a container filling up with water; suddenly, there would be a split second when the water came gushing and overflowing, and the moment had come.

It wasn't just that the time had come for Jesus. The time had come for the whole world, for the whole creation. As Jesus proclaimed, 'The kingdom of God is near.' An ancient Jewish prayer said, 'May God establish his kingdom in our lifetime.' Jesus was indicating that this prayer had been answered. The rule of God was near, and it was approaching. It was near in time and near in space—

so near, in fact, that it could be glimpsed, just as it was when Jesus entered the synagogue, taught with authority and carried out an exorcism. God's rule was taught and demonstrated; God's rule extended to the spiritual realm. Many religious Jews regarded the world as under the tyranny of Satan and evil—and now the liberator had arrived.

The whole of Jesus' ministry was characterized by his driving conviction that this was 'the time'. Where John had prepared, he was to fulfil. His birth had come when the time was right; now his life must be lived to announce, to explain and to demonstrate the reality of God's rule, so that his death would also come when the time was right, bringing salvation, new life and new hope.

Great God, you created the sun and moon by which we measure the passing of time. Help us to live our lives according to your time-keeping, knowing when you are prompting us, and using the time you have given to us in your service and for your glory. Amen.

30 December

NOT YET

After this, Jesus went around in Galilee, purposely staying away from Judea because the Jews there were waiting to take his life. But when the Jewish Feast of Tabernacles was near, Jesus' brothers said to him, 'You ought to leave here and go to Judea, so that your disciples may see the miracles you do. No one who wants to become a public figure acts in secret. Since you are doing these things, show yourself to the world.' For even his own brothers did not believe in him.

Therefore Jesus told them, 'The right time for me has not yet come; for you any time is right. The world cannot hate you, but it hates me because I testify that what it does is evil. You go to the Feast. I am not yet going up to this Feast, because for me the right time has not yet come.' Having said this, he stayed in Galilee. However, after his brothers had left for the Feast, he went also, not publicly, but in secret...

Then Jesus, still teaching in the temple courts, cried out, 'Yes, you know me, and you know where I am from. I am not here on my own, but he who sent me is true. You do not know him, but I know him because I am from him and he sent me.' At this they tried to seize him, but no one laid a hand on him, because his time had not yet come...

On the last and greatest day of the Feast, Jesus stood and said in a loud voice, 'If anyone is thirsty, let him come to me and drink. Whoever believes in me, as the Scripture has said, streams of living water will flow from within him.' By this he meant the Spirit, whom those who believed in him were later to receive. Up to that time the Spirit had not been given, since Jesus had not yet been glorified. On hearing his words, some of the people said, 'Surely this man is the Prophet.' Others said, 'He is the Christ.' Still others asked, 'How can the Christ come from Galilee? Does not the Scripture say that the Christ will come from David's family and from

Bethlehem, the town where David lived?' Thus the people were divided because of Jesus. Some wanted to seize him, but no one laid a hand on him.

JOHN 7:1–10, 28–30, 37–44

The secret of great comedy, we are told, is timing. The secret of understanding the ministry of Jesus, particularly in John's Gospel, is his sense of timing. It is the only way of making sense of John 7. This chapter, perhaps more than any other, reveals the way in which Jesus remained in control of his life under the authority of his Father.

The chapter begins with a statement that, in any other circumstances, would simply indicate that Jesus was afraid. Yet we know that this cannot be the explanation, because a short time later Jesus does go to Jerusalem, and faces his death with extraordinary courage and no sign of fear. There is perhaps a tiny clue in the use of the word 'purposely'. The translators are trying to give a hint of the explanation: the Greek word implies a definite strategic decision rather than a passing whim. Jesus would go to Jerusalem when his own knowledge of God's purposes told him that the time was right.

When his brothers try to persuade him to accompany them to celebrate the Feast of Tabernacles, he explicitly tells them that he is marching to the beat of a different drum: 'The right time for me has not yet come; for you any time is right.' His brothers' attempt at persuasion was based on a complete lack of understanding of Jesus' motivation and mission. Their judgment was less prophetic insight, more a modern B-list celebrity promotion. 'You've wowed the crowds here. Now go for Jerusalem. Today, Galilee; tomorrow, the world!' They seemed unaware of the danger, and unaware of Jesus' reluctance to abuse his miracle-making power for the sake of cheap popular appeal.

When they have gone, however, he changes his mind. Halfway through the feast he travels to Jerusalem, but arrives incognito. The statement is clear: he has taken control of his own destiny. There are echoes of Cana here. The wedding feast was on the edge of disaster when Mary prompted him to save the day. At first Jesus refused, on the same grounds: 'My time has not yet come' (John 2:4). Yet he then immediately performed the miracle. Again, it seems as if Jesus is making clear that he will act on God's direction, not at the prompting of his earthly family.

Jesus arrives in Jerusalem unrecognized, but nevertheless proceeds to the temple and begins teaching. He makes reference to the fact that they are trying to kill him, and the crowd are baffled, because they still do not know who he is, even though they are looking out for him. Jesus then challenges the crowd to stop judging 'by mere appearances' (v. 24), and some begin to realize just who is before them. At this point, Jesus reveals himself quite openly, and, as he anticipated, the temple guard move in—but they find themselves unable to take hold of him. Why? Because, John says, they are outside God's plan and purpose at that point: his time, his hour, has not yet come.

Now, I am a prosaic kind of person. I want to know why they couldn't lay a hand on him. John gives a theological answer, not a scientific one. Did Jesus disguise himself again, and lose himself in the crowd? We don't know. We know that God can give supernatural protection: he did it then, and he does it in the 21st century. Our problem is that he does not do it whenever we would like him to.

The Feast of Tabernacles lasted seven days, and was followed by a closing assembly. This was when Jesus chose to go public in a big way. Traditionally, teachers sat, and their pupils stood. But heralds also stood, making sure their voice could be heard above all the other noise. Standing at the very point where, for the last seven days, water has been brought from the Pool of Siloam and poured into a bowl by the altar, Jesus indicates that just as the time for that ritual is over for another year, it is time for the symbol to be replaced by the reality. He offers the living, eternal-life-giving water of the Spirit.

Notice, though, that timing still dominates. John is at pains to point out that Jesus was looking forward to the time when the Holy Spirit would be given, which could only happen after he had been 'glorified'. That was when his hour would come.

The boldness of his invitation divided his listeners, and it still does. It is baffling that people can still claim that Jesus was a good man, a great teacher, but that he wasn't divine. I'm convinced that they can never actually have read the Gospels. Jesus invites people to come to him for living water. Soon he will claim to be the light of the world. This is either madness, megalomania or divine truth. That's why it divides people. Jesus' listeners thought they knew where he was from, but they didn't. Even less did they understand where he was going. It wasn't his birthplace that was ultimately important: it was what he said and what he did. He was in control of his own destiny, and if you have assuaged your thirst with that living water, then he is in control of your destiny too. Your time will come. That's his promise.

Jesus, you are the light, the bread, the living water;
thank you for illumination, nourishment and refreshment
in the past year. Help me to thirst for you again in the coming year,
and drink deep of all that you offer to me. Amen.

31 December

SEIZE THE DAY

As the time approached for him to be taken up to heaven, Jesus resolutely set out for Jerusalem. And he sent messengers on ahead, who went into a Samaritan village to get things ready for him; but the people there did not welcome him, because he was heading for Jerusalem. When the disciples James and John saw this, they asked, 'Lord, do you want us to call fire down from heaven to destroy them?' But Jesus turned and rebuked them, and they went to another village.

As they were walking along the road, a man said to him, 'I will follow you wherever you go.' Jesus replied, 'Foxes have holes and birds of the air have nests, but the Son of Man has nowhere to lay his head.' He said to another man, 'Follow me.' But the man replied, 'Lord, first let me go and bury my father.' Jesus said to him, 'Let the dead bury their own dead, but you go and proclaim the kingdom of God.' Still another said, 'I will follow you, Lord; but first let me go back and say goodbye to my family.' Jesus replied, 'No one who puts his hand to the plough and looks back is fit for service in the kingdom of God.'

LUKE 9:51–62

It is New Year's Eve—quite a good day to think about Jesus at the start of a whole new period of his ministry, one in which Luke spells out what kind of commitment Jesus expects of his followers. Up until this moment, Jesus had been in Galilee, but now he is beginning his journey to Jerusalem: this section finishes with his entry into Jerusalem (19:28).

In the pattern of Luke's Gospel, this journey is explained by a reference back to the moment that, in one way, is the trigger for it. Jesus has climbed a hill with three of his closest friends and disciples; suddenly, his whole appearance is transformed. 'Two men, Moses and Elijah, appeared in glorious splendour, talking with Jesus. They spoke about his departure, which he was about to bring to fulfilment at Jerusalem' (Luke 9:30–31). The word 'departure' is the Greek word used for 'exodus': it conjures up a wonderful picture of Moses, Elijah and Jesus exchanging notes about journeys, about how God liberates people, about ways of getting from earth to heaven. Moses and Elijah were both taken into heaven in a way very similar to the ascension of Jesus—the difference being that Jesus went through the experience of death. Jesus' exodus journey was to include his death, his resurrection, and his ascension.

So now, says Luke, the time had come and the time was right. A literal translation of verse 51 is 'It was fulfilled that the time was fulfilled that he should be taken up.' There is a strong emphasis that one period is over and the next beginning, and, from the moment he sets out, it is a journey of destiny that will take him up—to Jerusalem, to a cross, and then to heaven. It is a package tour—but certainly no holiday. The original Greek in verse 51 doesn't mention heaven. Luke almost certainly intended that there should be a double layer of meaning: the Jews always regarded the journey for the festivals as 'going up to Jerusalem', and Moses and Elijah had been 'taken up' into heaven at the end of their earthly ministry.

There is even a resolution in this verse—not for a new year, but for this new phase of Jesus' life. He 'resolutely set out...' Literally, he 'fixed his face' or 'set his face' to go to Jerusalem. Like concrete, he was set firm for the journey, solid, immovable; his sight was set and focused on his goal. He was not to be diverted or distracted.

This might explain why he went by the direct route through Samaria, rather than diverting to avoid it, as many Galileans did. The hatred between Jews and Samaritans was mutual: the Jewish historian Josephus records an attack on Jewish pilgrims passing through Samaria that left many dead—an episode that no doubt reinforced the contempt and loathing heard in the words of James and John. They had just been with Elijah, the very man of God who had twice brought down fire on Samaritans (2 Kings 1:9–16). But Jesus is greater than Elijah: he does not have to follow the prophet's precedent. He has not come in judgment, but in love and mercy, to offer people an escape from judgment.

In the very next section, Jesus emphasizes his expectation of complete commitment. We live in a world where many see the most committed adherents of a faith as dangerous fanatics, so it is worth emphasizing the strong hint in this story that commitment to Jesus is not an excuse or a pretext for violent behaviour. We are not called to defend our faith by force. If we disagree, however strongly, with people and the policies they promote, we must always love them and respect them in our disagreements.

That is true in our families, our churches, our communities, and in our politics. I have been part of the campaign for debt cancellation for ten years or more; I am regarded as a 'political activist' by some. But when I established campaigning at Tearfund, I argued strongly that Christians should campaign in a distinctively Christian way. We encouraged people to send MPs cards congratulating them on their election, promising to pray for them and offering to work with them for the benefit of people who are poor. We urged that in all their dealings with politicians and civil servants, campaigners should show respect, be polite as well as firm, and always express thanks, particularly when action had been taken as suggested. I believe it is the right thing to do, and the right way of achieving change within the democracy that we enjoy. We need to demonstrate to the world that committed Christians are characterized by loving service in the community, not fanaticism, violence, bigotry and hate.

Jesus' challenge to commitment is not easy. He uses hyperbole to emphasize the extent to which his followers must put him first. He was not denying the Old Testament law that required people to honour their father and mother; he was indicating just how high on the priority list he had to come. It's worth noting, in passing, that the man who wanted to wait to bury his father might have waited a long time: if his father had just died, he would have been in the process of seeing to his burial. So he was, in effect, asking for permission to choose his own time to follow Jesus, when all other demands on him had been fulfilled.

Jesus is insistent. He can't promise comfort; he can't promise a home, or even a good night's sleep. But he can promise involvement in the work of the kingdom of God. Following Jesus is not about taking a stroll through the fields of religious belief. It is about getting stuck in to the task of changing the world and helping to answer the prayer we know so well: 'Your kingdom come, your will be done.' As *THE MESSAGE* translates Luke 9:62, 'No procrastination. No backward looks. You can't put God's kingdom off till tomorrow. Seize the day.' How about that for a New Year's resolution?

Lord of the years, we bring our thanks today.
We thank you for all that is past.
We thank you for all that lies ahead.
Amen.

1 January

THE FULL EXTENT OF LOVE

It was just before the Passover Feast. Jesus knew that the time had come for him to leave this world and go to the Father. Having loved his own who were in the world, he now showed them the full extent of his love. The evening meal was being served, and the devil had already prompted Judas Iscariot, son of Simon, to betray Jesus. Jesus knew that the Father had put all things under his power, and that he had come from God and was returning to God; so he got up from the meal, took off his outer clothing, and wrapped a towel round his waist. After that, he poured water into a basin and began to wash his disciples' feet, drying them with the towel that was wrapped round him...

When he had finished washing their feet, he put on his clothes and returned to his place. 'Do you understand what I have done for you?' he asked them. 'You call me "Teacher" and "Lord", and rightly so, for that is what I am. Now that I, your Lord and Teacher, have washed your feet, you also should wash one another's feet. I have set you an example that you should do as I have done for you. I tell you the truth, servants are not greater than their masters, nor are messengers greater than the one who sent them. Now that you know these things, you will be blessed if you do them.'

JOHN 13:1–5,12–17

Here's a great thought on the first day of a new year: what would you do if you were told you only had a few days to live? There's one obvious and completely understandable reaction—after you had got over the initial shock—and one you often hear of in the newspapers: you would try to do at least some of the things you had always wanted to do. In 2003, the BBC showed a television programme called *Fifty things to do before you die*, based on the opinions of 20,000 viewers. What do you think was on the list? There was bungee-jumping, white-water rafting, paragliding and climbing Everest; seeing elephants, polar bears, tigers, whales and gorillas in the wild; travelling to Machu Picchu, the Great Wall of China, the Pyramids (by camel) and New York by Concorde (whoops, too late); but the top choice was swimming with dolphins!

I have already done a very few of the fifty, and would not say no to a few others. The ones I have done, I have enjoyed enormously and have recommended them to friends. My wife's absolute favourite was number 27 on the programme, 'wonder at a waterfall': the best value-for-money bargain I ever got (as far as she is concerned) was a hotel room overlooking the Niagara Falls. But of course, what all fifty activities have in common—wonderful experiences all—is that they are of benefit to *me*; they are all about what *I* get out of them. There's nothing wrong with them—there are far worse ambitions to have—but they reflect a world where increasing wealth brings an increasing range of possibilities within our reach, and what used to be a rare and precious indulgence becomes a package holiday excursion. Have you noticed how much harder it gets to buy Christmas presents each year? What do you give to the one who has everything?

Not surprisingly, Jesus offers us a slightly different perspective. His time had come. He was preparing to leave the world, facing his death. I'm not sure exactly how much the awareness of resurrection and ascension would have affected his emotions at this particular time. The garden of Gethsemane is close by, where the indications of stress suggest a very real sense of deep apprehension at the impending experience of suffering and death (Luke 22:44). The film *The Passion of the Christ* certainly conveyed the awful physical pain and torture that Jesus endured, but I wonder how much greater was the spiritual suffering of separation from his Father while bearing the punishment for the sins of the world.

Yet, at the very moment when he had most reason to be withdrawn and concerned about himself, Jesus was thinking of others, prepared to give them his time and to serve them. Did any of the people surveyed by the BBC for their programme want to do something significant for someone else among their 'fifty things'—to make sure they left the world a better place because they had lived? There can be no greater pressure than a sentence of death: sometimes it is said that when someone is under real pressure, it is the real person that is revealed.

John writes that, under the greatest pressure of his life, Jesus 'showed them the full extent of his love', and then he washed their feet. At first sight, this is a little puzzling: surely washing feet was not the full extent of Jesus' love for his friends? There are two possible explanations for this slightly strange juxtaposition. The first is that John is introducing the whole final section of his Gospel here, so that the 'full extent of his love' is shown from the moment of washing the disciples' feet right up until he says 'It is finished' and gives up his spirit (John 19:30): 'Greater love has no one than this, to lay down one's life for one's friends' (John 15:13). The other possibility is that the emphasis is on the idea of 'showing' his love, so washing their feet was a demonstration, an explanation, of what the full extent of his love really was. Both possibilities are right, I suspect.

The explanation of the foot-washing is given great emphasis: Jesus did not necessarily want his followers to be ready literally to wash the feet of others; he wanted them to follow his example. As Paul puts it, 'Your attitude should be the same as that of Christ Jesus' (Philippians 2:5). Foot-washing revealed the attitude that Jesus wants his followers to live out in their words and actions. John carefully indicates that Jesus knew he had power, but used it in service of others. John also highlights the presence of Judas among the gathering—but this is no excuse for refusing to serve. Jesus loves and serves his enemies as well as his friends.

In his first letter, John returns to the idea that the sacrificial love of Jesus is not a blessing but an example: 'This is how we know what love is: Jesus Christ laid down his life for us. And we ought to lay down our lives for one another. If anyone of you has material possessions and sees a brother or sister in need but has no pity on them, how can the love of God be in you? Dear children, let us not love with words or tongue but with actions and in truth' (1 John 3:16–18).

The first challenge is to follow Jesus' example in how we relate to our fellow Christians—and I know just how hard that can be! But the reference to messengers in John 13:16 indicates that as we take the message of the love of Jesus, the one who sends us, out into the world, we must follow the example of the one who 'so loved the world that he gave his one and only Son' (John 3:16).

It may not be a question of fifty things to do before we die, but on 1 January there is certainly a question about what our priorities will be for this year. How will we follow the example of Jesus? Whose feet need washing?

Lord, this year I want to serve you.
Lord, this year I want to serve you in serving others.
Lord, this year I want to move on with you.
Lord, make this year different because you have made me different.
I give this year to you. I give myself to you.
Amen.

2 January

TIME FOR GLORY

After Jesus said this, he looked towards heaven and prayed: 'Father, the time has come. Glorify your Son, that your Son may glorify you. For you granted him authority over all people that he might give eternal life to all those you have given him. Now this is eternal life: that they may know you, the only true God, and Jesus Christ, whom you have sent. I have brought you glory on earth by completing the work you gave me to do. And now, Father, glorify me in your presence with the glory I had with you before the world began...

'My prayer is not for them alone. I pray also for those who will believe in me through their message, that all of them may be one, Father, just as you are in me and I am in you. May they also be in us so that the world may believe that you have sent me. I have given them the glory that you gave me, that they may be one as we are one: I in them and you in me. May they be brought to complete unity to let the world know that you sent me and have loved them even as you have loved me. Father, I want those you have given me to be with me where I am, and to see my glory, the glory you have given me because you loved me before the creation of the world.'

JOHN 17:1–5, 20–24

As the divine clock ticks on towards the moment of redemption of the whole universe, we discover that the death of Jesus is far more even than an act of sacrificial love. It is also, extraordinarily, a moment of glory. Human history has seen many moments when death and glory have been linked: Pheidippides running from the battlefield at Marathon to Athens and dying as he gave news of victory; the charge of the Light Brigade in the Crimean War; Nelson at the battle of Trafalgar.

These examples are all associated with warfare, and the death of Jesus is the key moment of victory in the spiritual war that has raged since the serpent first suggested rebellion in the garden of Eden—but it takes the eye of faith to see that. The onlookers who mocked and jeered on the day of the crucifixion of Jesus saw a bloodied body, helpless and racked with pain, dying as a common criminal. The hardened Roman officer in charge of the execution was the closest, however, and he saw something different: 'And when the centurion, who stood there in front of Jesus, heard his cry and saw how he died, he said, "Surely this man was the Son of God!"' (Mark 15:39). He had a glimpse of glory.

It is clear that in his prayer Jesus is referring to his impending death, although part of the reason he can envisage his death as glorifying God is that it will be inseparable from his resurrection, ascension and rule over the kingdom of God. The typical route to glory for Roman emperors was to win a great battle and return to Rome in triumph for a glorious coronation. But in this prayer Jesus is not looking forward to the glory of heaven for himself so much as the fact that he is about to make it possible for people to know God, receive eternal life and share the glory of heaven with him.

The cross of Jesus is far more than a personal triumph over death; it is a cosmic triumph over sin and evil, and it produces fruit: 'Jesus replied, "The hour has come for the Son of Man to be glorified. I tell you the truth, unless a grain of wheat falls to the ground and dies, it remains only a single seed. But if it dies, it produces many seeds' (John 12:23–24). The same thought is reflected in the wording of his appeal to God—'Glorify your Son, that your Son may glorify you'—which is followed by an echo, the same idea in different words: 'For you granted him authority over all people that he might give eternal life to all those you have given him' (John 17:1–2). Jesus' death is the key that unlocks his authority. The purpose of his being glorified, of being given authority, is that people can receive eternal life and Jesus can thus glorify his Father.

Those whom the Father had given him were to take his love and share his message. Jesus' final words to his disciples refer back to the words in the prayer of John 17: 'All authority in heaven and on earth has been given to me. Therefore go and make disciples of all nations, baptizing them in the name of the Father and of the Son and of the Holy Spirit, and teaching them to obey everything I have commanded you. And surely I am with you always, to the very end of the age' (Matthew 28:18–20).

In Jesus' mind, also, there is a link between the disciples carrying forward his mission and being bound together in unity: 'May they be brought to complete unity to let the world know that you sent me' (John 17:23). In one sense, it is obvious. If Christians can't even treat one another kindly, it scarcely commends the love of God that they claim to know. From experience, we all know many people who are put off God by the behaviour of Christians in general, and specifically by signs of division in the church and the plethora of denominations.

Yet it is not as simple as saying that all churches must unite. I don't think Jesus had organizational unity in mind when he prayed this prayer. Diversity is not the same as division. It is good that there are churches that allow people to worship in their own language; churches for the extroverts and the introverts; churches offering noisy, exuberant charismatic worship, and contemplative liturgy complete with choral plainsong.

What's more, it is clear that as the early church grew and spread, Paul had to wrestle with a very real problem: how do you maintain the unity of the church and at the same time ensure that the truth of the gospel is not being distorted by false teaching? In his letters, he is constantly urging believers to agree, on the one hand (see 1 Corinthians 1:10; Philippians 4:2), and on the other to have nothing to do with those who do not teach the truth (2 Corinthians 11:12–13; Galatians 1:6–9). Part of the problem is, of course, that we find it far easier to fall out with people than to agree with them over who has the right understanding of the truth.

We have to ensure that we do not make our personal preferences (over styles of worship, Bible versions, what we wear in church, and so on) into touchstones of doctrinal purity. Neither must we let our genuine disagreements with others become reasons for ceasing to love and care for them. Even as I write this, I am searching my own conscience. Long ago I was asked to leave a church and, more recently, left another at a point where I felt I could not continue there any longer. I have experienced the pain and heartache and hurt that it brings—and this prayer of Jesus indicates that he shares in all those emotions.

We need to keep praying together, working together and serving together, bound together with a vision of God's glory that is ours to share in mission in this world, and to experience in the presence of Jesus in the next. We need to reflect on this prayer of Jesus—'Now my heart is troubled, and what shall I say? "Father, save me from this hour"? No, it was for this very reason I came to this hour. Father, glorify your name!'—and the Father's reply: 'I have glorified it, and will glorify it again' (John 12:27–28).

Lord God, head of the church,
grant that we may be given grace to love our fellow Christians.
Grant that they may be given grace to love us.
Glorify your name in your church,
for Jesus' sake. Amen.

3 January

EATING AND SLEEPING

He replied, 'Go into the city to a certain man and tell him, "The Teacher says: My appointed time is near. I am going to celebrate the Passover with my disciples at your house."' So the disciples did as Jesus had directed them and prepared the Passover...

While they were eating, Jesus took bread, gave thanks and broke it, and gave it to his disciples, saying, 'Take and eat; this is my body.' Then he took the cup, gave thanks and offered it to them, saying, 'Drink from it, all of you. This is my blood of the covenant, which is poured out for many for the forgiveness of sins.' ...

Then Jesus went with his disciples to a place called Gethsemane, and he said to them, 'Sit here while I go over there and pray.' He took Peter and the two sons of Zebedee along with him, and he began to be sorrowful and troubled. Then he said to them, 'My soul is overwhelmed with sorrow to the point of death. Stay here and keep watch with me.' Going a little farther, he fell with his face to the ground and prayed, 'My Father, if it is possible, may this cup be taken from me. Yet not as I will, but as you will.'

Then he returned to his disciples and found them sleeping. 'Couldn't you keep watch with me for one hour?' he asked Peter. 'Watch and pray so that you will not fall into temptation. The spirit is willing, but the body is weak.' He went away a second time and prayed, 'My Father, if it is not possible for this cup to be taken away unless I drink it, may your will be done.' When he came back, he again found them sleeping, because their eyes were heavy. So he left them and went away once more and prayed the third time, saying the same thing. Then he returned to the disciples and said to them, 'Are you still sleeping and resting? Look, the hour is near, and the Son of Man is betrayed into the hands of sinners.'

MATTHEW 26:18–19, 26–28, 36–45

Jerusalem at Passover time: packed with people, thousands camping outside the walls, and the aroma of roast lamb filling the air. Jesus is acutely aware that time is running out, and wants his disciples to share with him in a last meal—and a first communion. In one sense, of course, in Jewish culture as in so many cultures across the world today, a proper meal is always one that is shared, that builds relationship, that encourages fellowship. What better way of creating and celebrating friendship than by eating together?

Sometimes, meals are memorable for the food—whether it is so delicious, so exotic, or so awful! The book I wrote about my travels with Tearfund was called *Guinea Pig for Lunch* because I really did eat guinea pig for lunch. It was a memorable day on the top of the Andes, where guinea pig is a highly valued part of the regular diet, the native Indian population having bred them for food for centuries. My daughters—then quite young, and proud owners of Crackle the guinea pig—were not over-impressed by this argument, especially when Crackle died shortly after my return. But the title did help to sell the book!

A beautifully prepared and well-presented meal is a complete delight. I make no excuses for enjoying my food, while remaining committed to the task of trying to ensure that everyone in God's world can eat a healthy meal every day. Some of my most fondly remembered meals were shared with those who had given almost everything they had to offer me hospitality—and it is the company that matters. I'm famous (or notorious?) in my family for my obsession with collecting newspaper vouchers that allow good meals at reasonable prices. We've used them in some very posh restaurants: I feel I have brought Susan a long way since I first took her out to the Wimpy Bar in the Mile End Road, East London, in 1969. We have a family tradition that on Mum and Dad's birthdays (two days apart), the family have a meal together—with vouchers—because we are family.

Susan and I have tried to make this a feature of church life too, precisely because church should have the best features of a family. To me, it's obvious: sharing a meal is a way of sharing life together. Even the word 'fellowship', which churches love to use, is a translation of the Greek word for sharing a meal, *koinonia*. In our present church, eating together is a regular feature. I might even dare to say that it is part of our worship. In the last year or so, we've also extended the idea to our street, using the idea of a fellowship meal to nurture a sense of local community. We knocked on every door to invite our neighbours to our first street barbecue. We had lived in the street for 24 years; we met a gentleman a few doors down who had been a resident for at least twice as long, whom we had never seen before. People came around 3pm, and at 8pm they suggested relighting the barbecue and having supper—which we did, out on the pavement with the baby alarms lined up on the garden walls.

Community and communion: the words are more closely related than we might think. One theologian has commented that communion started as a big meal with a little symbolism, and the church has made it a little meal with big symbolism. The ideal must be for the church to enjoy the physical, emotional, social and spiritual dimensions of communion with God and one another. It is then a means of grace, of receiving something of God and from God, in every sense. The reality and the symbolism are beautiful and enriching: broken bread for a body broken, so that his body, the church, could be brought together; the cup of wine for blood shed in death, so that we could know the forgiveness of sins and receive new life.

When the time came, Jesus found a quiet place among the crowds to prepare for the ordeal ahead. He looked for support from his closest friends, but the meal, the wine and the heat were too much for them. Do you know the feeling? How often the spirit is willing but the body is weak! My ability to fall asleep anywhere is legendary: invigilating a school exam; in a dugout canoe with my chin leaning on an open umbrella; on a train in Bangladesh; on church steps in Ethiopia; during Acts 2, 4 and 5 of *Hamlet* one warm summer's evening; even during several sermons, though not one of my own—yet. I pray, though, that I won't be caught napping at the moment Jesus has a vital task for me to do. And if human beings are made in

God's image, then I pray too that I'll be alert to the opportunities that strangers and neighbours present to me to serve Jesus by being open to and meeting their needs.

In the garden of Gethsemane, we see Jesus wrestling with the cost of obedience to his Father: while the disciples are overwhelmed by tiredness, he is overwhelmed with sorrow. Sometimes, when we take the communion cup, we could do worse than echo his prayer: 'not my will, but yours be done'. He died to give us life, so that we could share in his embracing of his Father's will and purpose. For when Jesus took the cup, he promised, 'I will not drink of this fruit of the vine from now on until that day when I drink it anew with you in my Father's kingdom' (Matthew 26:29). There's a date in the diary. It's for a feast, a heavenly banquet—with the best surroundings, the best food, the best background music and, above all, the best company. What's more, the price has been paid.

Loving Father,
we praise you for the joy of sharing meals together.
We praise you for bread and wine that speaks of sacrifice and new life.
We praise you for the expectation of a great feast in heaven.
Help us to be people who share, who contribute
to community and fellowship in every way.
For all that we have received, we are truly thankful.
Amen.

4 January

NOW IS THE TIME TO WORSHIP

Jesus asked her, 'Would you please give me a drink of water?' 'You are a Jew,' she replied, 'and I am a Samaritan woman. How can you ask me for a drink of water when Jews and Samaritans won't have anything to do with each other?' Jesus answered, 'You don't know what God wants to give you, and you don't know who is asking you for a drink. If you did, you would ask me for the water that gives life... Everyone who drinks this water will get thirsty again. But no one who drinks the water I give will ever be thirsty again. The water I give is like a flowing fountain that gives eternal life.'

The woman said, 'Sir, I can see that you are a prophet. My ancestors worshiped on this mountain, but you Jews say Jerusalem is the only place to worship.' Jesus said to her: 'Believe me, the time is coming when you won't worship the Father either on this mountain or in Jerusalem. You Samaritans don't really know the one you worship. But we Jews do know the God we worship, and by using us, God will save the world. But a time is coming, and it is already here! Even now the true worshipers are being led by the Spirit to worship the Father according to the truth. These are the ones the Father is seeking to worship him. God is Spirit, and those who worship God must be led by the Spirit to worship him according to the truth.'

The woman said, 'I know that the Messiah will come. He is the one we call Christ. When he comes, he will explain everything to us.' 'I am that one,' Jesus told her, 'and I am speaking to you now.'

JOHN 4:8–26 (CEV, ABRIDGED)

I once spent a wonderful few minutes surrounded by a group of laughing and giggling women. It was the kind of laughter that is good-natured and infectious, that creates its own oasis of happiness. They were standing round a well in West Africa, on the edge of the Sahara desert, watching a very pasty white-skinned, middle-aged man hauling a bucket of water up out of the depths. I was that man. It was hot, it was hard work, and I have no idea why they found it so funny. My guess is that they may never have seen a man engaged in this activity before. They may even have wondered why I did not do the obvious thing that any passing male visitor would do—ask one of them to draw a bucket of water so that I could have a drink.

All over the developing world, wells are women's territory: they walk, they do the hard work, they have a chat and exchange news. So what was Jesus doing at a well? He was certainly living dangerously. He was talking to a woman; he was talking to a Samaritan woman; he was talking to a woman by herself; he was talking to a woman with a 'history'. How many social, cultural and religious taboos could he break in one conversation?

It is reasonably clear from the story that Jesus' prophetic insight into the intimate detail of the woman's personal life ('You have already been married five times, and the man you are now living with isn't your husband') made her anxious to change the subject. But maybe she really was interested in issues about worship. When I ran Alpha courses, I knew that I needed spiritual discernment to know whether to follow a red herring in the conversation or whether to leave it. Most of the time, I gave people the benefit of the doubt: if they asked a question, they deserved an answer—even the person who asked me via our church website what our view was of vampires! All too often, the church decides that the question, or even the questioner, is not worth an answer. What a tragedy! Jesus valued this woman and her questions; he may have been the first person to do so for a very long time.

Not too long ago, our home group studied the Gospel of John. It made us ask some hard questions too! Getting to grips with the Bible takes real effort. We should praise God for the parts that are easy to understand, but never be afraid of what looks more difficult—and beware of what seems simple, but isn't! It's vital to explore what the passage was intended to say to its original hearers; when that's clear, it is much easier to think how to apply it to our own situation. As the home group leader, I wrestled with the passage, and I wrestled with the books about the passage—and I had what for me was a real insight: John's account describes Jesus blowing apart all the deepest convictions that people held about the way to know and be accepted by God.

In John 3, Jesus meets Nicodemus and tells him, 'You must be born again'. Why? Because he wanted to say that being born a Jew was not the qualification for knowing God. Two thousand years later, millions of people are sure that their religion is decided by their birth, and Jesus still says, 'You must be born again' (John 3:7). In John 5:39–40, he challenges the belief that the key to religion is in a holy book: 'You diligently study the Scriptures because you think that by them you possess eternal life. These are the Scriptures that testify about me, yet you refuse to come to me to have life.' And in between these two chapters, he meets the woman at the well and discusses whether God can only be known in a particular place. Is it Mount Gerizim, as the Samaritans claimed, or Jerusalem, as the Jews insisted? 'It's neither,' says Jesus; 'where we worship is not the key to knowing God.' This is the astonishing reality in the message of Jesus: it's not our parentage, our holy book or our temple that matters. It's all about him, because 'I am the way and the truth and the life. No one comes to the Father except through me' (John 14:6).

My wife Susan used to be responsible for the prayer meeting before the Sunday services, where a faithful few would gather each week and ask for God's blessing on all who gathered and all that was to take place. One of the most faithful was also one of the most repetitive: every week, almost without fail, he would pray that we would worship 'in spirit and in truth'. Agreed—but what does it mean? A whole book could be written, but here is what I think is the essence of this revolutionary statement.

First, God's Spirit inspires and informs our worship, and our spirits respond. Ultimately, worship is not the words or the music, the surroundings, the liturgy, the silence, or the posture: it is the reality of God's spirit meeting with our spirit. The other aspects are either encouragements or hindrances: they are enormously important, but they are definitely not worship in themselves. We can fall in love with worship, just as we can fall in love with the Bible, but both are intended to lead us to the true object of our love: Jesus himself.

This is part of what it means to worship in truth. If we focus only on the ritual, the formalities (or informalities) and the outward trappings, we cannot worship in truth. It's a little like endlessly polishing the car but never using it to go anywhere. What's more, we need to make sure our worship is rooted in the objective truth about God revealed in the Bible: we worship God because of his power, his love, his justice, his goodness, his greatness, his closeness. We didn't make these things up. That's why turning scripture into worship is so rewarding: it helps us all to grow in our knowledge of God.

Next, the Bible is abundantly clear that we can only worship God in truth when our actions match our words. Religious services can make God sick. 'When you spread out your hands in prayer, I will hide my eyes from you; even if you offer many prayers, I will not listen. Your hands are full of blood; wash and make yourselves clean. Take your evil deeds out of my sight! Stop doing wrong, learn to do right! Seek justice, encourage the oppressed. Defend the cause of the fatherless, plead the case of the widow' (Isaiah 1:15–17). The truth of our worship in a church service will be revealed by the service we do during the rest of the week.

Finally, we need to worship in the full recognition of the truth about ourselves. There is no room for pretence when we meet with God. It's pointless: we can't fool ourselves and we certainly can't fool God. So who are we trying to fool? Am I really more worried about what other people think than what God thinks? That's a dangerous place to be. At the start of a new year, let's commit to being honest with God about ourselves, and sincere in our search for his truth through his word. When the woman by the well told Jesus the truth, he revealed his truth to her. 'I am the one,' he said.

Fill us with your Spirit, O God.
May our worship honour you,
because what we are is true,
because what we say is true,
and because what we do is true to our words and your word.
Amen.

5–6 JANUARY

THE TIME IS COMING

INTRODUCTION

The story of Advent is the story of God's master plan. First hinted at in the judgment on sin in the garden of Eden, we have traced it down through history until a baby is born in a manger. We have seen it fulfilled when that baby grows up to accomplish his own destiny through death, resurrection and ascension into heaven—and then sends his Spirit so that his people can be set free to worship in spirit and in truth.

The story of Advent is therefore also the story of how we are all called to play our part in God's purposes as we are born again by the Spirit of God.

Even that is not the end of the story, however. As the disciples stood gazing into the heavens as Jesus disappeared from their sight, they were given a final message: 'This same Jesus, who has been taken from you into heaven, will come back in the same way you have seen him go into heaven' (Acts 1:11). The first Advent was always a means to an end—the final restoration of the *shalom* so tragically and comprehensively shattered by sin in the garden of Eden. This final restoration will be established by the return of the king, the one who is worthy to reign for ever and ever.

In Hebrews, we read, 'Christ was sacrificed once to take away the sins of many people; and he will appear a second time, not to bear sin, but to bring salvation to those who are waiting for him' (9:28) There is no full stop at the end of time. There is joy, there is peace, there's a wedding feast. Children may light the Advent candles and look forward to presents, but the real Advent expectation is the light of his presence.

5 January

THE TRUMPET SHALL SOUND

My friends, we want you to understand how it will be for those followers who have already died. Then you won't grieve over them and be like people who don't have any hope. We believe that Jesus died and was raised to life. We also believe that when God brings Jesus back again, he will bring with him all who had faith in Jesus before they died. Our Lord Jesus told us that when he comes, we won't go up to meet him ahead of his followers who have already died.

With a loud command and with the shout of the chief angel and a blast of God's trumpet, the Lord will return from heaven. Then those who had faith in Christ before they died will be raised to life. Next, all of us who are still alive will be taken up into the clouds together with them to meet the Lord in the sky. From that time on we will all be with the Lord forever. Encourage each other with these words. I don't need to write to you about the time or date when all this will happen. You surely know that the Lord's return will be as a thief coming at night.

1 THESSALONIANS 4:13—5:2 (CEV)

My ram's-horn trumpet is a treasured possession. It is a small, pocket-sized (just), wonderfully smooth *shofar*, and when I blow it properly it produces an inspiring sound. 'But why?' I hear you ask. When I was first involved in Jubilee 2000 (now Jubilee Debt Campaign), the campaign for the cancellation of the unpayable debt of the world's poorest countries under a fair and transparent process, there was, not surprisingly, much interest in the meaning of 'jubilee'. My research revealed that one likely origin was from the Hebrew word used for the sound of the ram's-horn trumpet. The reason was simple: 'On the Great Day of Forgiveness sound the trumpet throughout your land. Consecrate the fiftieth year and proclaim liberty throughout the land to all its inhabitants. It shall be a jubilee for you' (Leviticus 25:9–10, CEV).

The year of Jubilee was enshrined in God's law as a time of intervention on behalf of the poor. Every fifty years, the trumpet would sound and herald a new start—new hope for those who were in debt and destitute. Imagine that you were one of those struggling against the odds, every meal eked out of back-breaking labour on unresponsive soil, but knowing that there was a promise of a new start. Your ears would have strained for the sound, the moment when things would change. When Jesus began his public ministry, he referred to this same moment as he quoted Isaiah: 'The Spirit of the Lord is upon me, because he has anointed me to bring good news to the poor' (Luke 4:18). Then, in one of the most dramatic moments in the whole of the Bible, Jesus began his sermon, 'Today this scripture is fulfilled in your hearing' (v. 21). In effect, he was saying, 'The trumpet has sounded.'

The trumpet blast is the sound that announces God's intervention in human history. This is why jubilee became the inspiration for a movement that longed for a new start for the world's poor: to celebrate the start of a new millennium by setting them free from the chains of debt. Jubilee 2000 set out to change the world, and its story is a testament to the power of biblical inspiration to motivate ordinary people to make a difference. A hard-bitten journalist was moved to write in *The Observer* that at the end of the 20th century it was the Bible, not Karl Marx, that had turned out to have more power to change history.

History has been changed. World poverty is on the global agenda as never before. In 2000, all world leaders agreed at the United Nations to take action to halve poverty by 2015, by signing up to the Millennium Development Goals. The Make Poverty History campaign in 2005 saw millions of people wearing a white band as a sign of their commitment to this cause; the leaders of the world's richest countries met in Scotland, and, even with the awful distraction of terrorist bombs in London, agreed to make significant steps forward to combat poverty in Africa. Much debt has been cancelled, and this has made a vital difference in many countries, with more children able to go to school, more vaccinations given, more clinics staffed by nurses and stocked with medicine. There is more to do, of course: as long as a child dies every three seconds because of extreme poverty, as a result of disease and malnutrition that are easily preventable, then Christians must remain at the fore-front of the battle for justice, and keep working to hear the sound of the jubilee trumpet.

I have blown my ram's-horn trumpet outside the World Bank, the Treasury buildings in London and in Washington. It has been suggested that I should have walked round the buildings for seven days and then blown the trumpet, to see whether I could replicate the Jericho effect. But I was not trying to destroy their walls: I was intending to add to the occasion an audible representation of the presence of a God who cares for the poor, who demands that justice is done, and who does not leave human history to hurtle on to destruction.

One day, the sound will be heard again, to herald the second Advent, to announce the second coming of Christ: 'the trumpet will sound, and the dead will be raised' (1 Corinthians 15:52, NIV). Paul wrote these words to reassure people who were growing increasingly concerned that, as time passed, more and more of their Christian family would die and therefore miss out on the much-anticipated second coming of Jesus. He did not want them to grieve as if they had no hope for the future, so he emphasizes that the trumpet blast will be heard alike by all Christians, whether alive or dead. The promise is that all who have faith in Jesus will be guaranteed life, and that life will be with Jesus: 'Christ died for us, so that we could live with him, whether we are alive or dead when he comes' (1 Thessalonians 5:10, CEV).

There was one other vital question: when was God going to act? Paul didn't need to tell the Thessalonian Christians the answer. Perhaps they had heard what Jesus had said to the apostles the last time they spoke together: 'They asked, "Master, are you going to restore the kingdom to Israel now? Is this the time?" He told them, "You don't get to know the time. Timing is the Father's business. What you'll get is the Holy Spirit"' (Acts 1:6–8, *THE MESSAGE*). It is incredible how much time Christians have spent, trying to work out what Jesus himself said he didn't know: the date of the second coming. In almost every generation there have been those who gave untold hours to arcane research and announced the result (curiously, nearly always in the relatively near future), only for bitter disappointment, sometimes great tragedy, to follow when the day passed.

Many believers have given up on the reality because they can't know the date. The longer the wait, some argue, the less likely it is to happen at all. This is a slightly strange conclusion for people of faith to make! After all, the faithful had waited expectantly for generation after generation for the first Advent. Some had given up hope, but one day it happened. A baby was born in a stable, heralded by a choir of angels heard by only a few. The promise is that the second coming will happen. It will be a global event: we won't even need round-the-clock television news to tell us, because the trumpet will sound.

God of justice,
God who intervenes in human history on behalf of the poor,
as we look forward to the sound of your trumpet
to announce the return of your Son,
help us to be instruments of your justice in your world
and sound the trumpet of your freedom.
In Jesus' name. Amen.

6 January

ADVENT LIVES

With God, one day is as good as a thousand years, a thousand years as a day. God isn't late with his promise as some measure lateness. He is restraining himself on account of you, holding back the End because he doesn't want anyone lost. He's giving everyone space and time to change. But when the Day of God's Judgment does come, it will be unannounced, like a thief. The sky will collapse with a thunderous bang, everything disintegrating in a huge conflagration, earth and all its works exposed to the scrutiny of Judgment.

Since everything here today might well be gone tomorrow, do you see how essential it is to live a holy life? Daily expect the Day of God, eager for its arrival. The galaxies will burn up and the elements melt down that day—but we'll hardly notice. We'll be looking the other way, ready for the promised new heavens and the promised new earth, all landscaped with righteousness. So, my dear friends, since this is what you have to look forward to, do your very best to be found living at your best, in purity and peace. Interpret our Master's patient restraint for what it is: salvation.
2 PETER 3:8–15 (*THE MESSAGE*)

Peter picks up where Paul left off in yesterday's reading. The fact that Jesus has not returned, he says, is not because God has forgotten, or called it off, or is running late with so many other things to do. It is out of his love and mercy for the human race: he longs so much for people to be in fellowship with him that he wants to give as much time as possible for individuals to turn to him, to discover the possibility of knowing him—because when Jesus returns as king, he returns to bring justice.

It's a serious matter. One word in English translation has had enormous impact. It could be translated 'justice', or it could be translated 'judgment'—but what a different ring 'Justice Day' has, compared to 'Judgment Day'. The promise is that Jesus will come and do the right thing. Those who have trusted him, served him and longed to know him will be welcomed into his presence just as they welcome his presence. Those who have never wanted to know him, who have rejected his love and care, will discover that justice confirms their choice: his presence will not be forced on to them for the whole of eternity.

The Greek word most frequently used for the second Advent of Jesus is *parousia*. It means 'coming', but it also means 'presence'. In one sense, we can understand that: the vital thing for the New Testament writers was not so much that he was coming again, but that when he came he would be with them, and they with him. There would be no more separation. Our younger daughter Helen has always enjoyed coming to the airport to meet me off a plane when I come home from a trip away. Part of it, I am confident, is because she is pleased to see me; but I know that she also enjoys watching the excitement of others as long-awaited friends and family are greeted with hugs and whoops of joy. The arrival matters because of the presence that follows—and you can't have the presence without the arrival.

Today is Epiphany. As a Christian festival, it is linked to all kinds of traditions and meanings in different parts of the world. 6 January has been celebrated as Christmas Day, as a festival for the Baptism of Jesus and the Trinity—since Jesus' baptism was a moment when all three persons of the Trinity were represented: the Father spoke, the Son was baptized, and the Holy Spirit descended as a dove. The day carries a strong tradition, too, of marking the 'shining forth' of God in the person of Jesus, the fulfilment of the Jewish festival of lights. And, of course, many associate the day with the coming of the magi.

'Epiphany' comes from the Greek word meaning 'to show, to make an appearance'. My well-thumbed dictionary tells me that it means 'moment of manifestation of supernatural reality'. That's an apt description of the scene when these visitors from a far-off country knelt and worshipped a baby. I praise God for every epiphany experience: for each time that I've seen God at work in people's lives, as well as my own; for every miracle of people coming to see and know Jesus for themselves; for every 'moment of manifestation of supernatural reality'. At the start of a new year, it is always positive to look back and recognize those moments in the past year, and to pray for many more in the year to come.

Every time the word 'epiphany' is used in the New Testament, though, it is a reference to the second Advent of Jesus. Paul is confident, for example, that because of what Jesus did through his first Advent he can look forward with great expectation: 'Now there is in store for me the crown of righteousness, which the Lord, the righteous Judge, will award to me on that day—and not only to me, but also to all who have longed for his appearing' (2 Timothy 4:8).

As we have looked, during this Advent and Christmas season, at the way God works out his purposes through human history, it's wholly appropriate that we should finish by considering not only God's final intervention in time when Jesus returns, but also what it has to say to us and about our lives. Peter wanted to encourage his readers to make sure they would be found living at their best. The life of the Christian is an anticipation of the kingdom of heaven.

When someone really important is coming to visit, we make sure we are ready: food in the fridge, house tidy, bed made. We are prepared. We want to be ready to enjoy the visitor's presence. My problem is that I always leave these preparations until the last minute. When we have guests for dinner in the evening, I am often still in the bath when the doorbell rings. Perhaps that is exactly why God has not let me know the date: 'So, my disciples, always be ready! You don't know the day or the time when all this will happen' (Matthew 25:13, CEV). I need to live my life so that I'm ready every day. But then, the message of Advent is that Jesus can be born into our lives and we can know his presence by his Spirit. If we are living our lives as though it were Christmas every day, then the world will be blessed, we'll be blessed—and we'll be ready.

Loving Father, creator of the universe, author of salvation,
thank you for all that the first Advent has meant
for the world, and has meant for me.
I want to celebrate the life you have given me to live,
by living it for you and the people you have made;
I want to celebrate this life in anticipation of the second Advent
and of the life to come.
Even so, Lord, come. Amen.

Our Master, Jesus Christ, is on his way.
He'll show up right on time,
his arrival guaranteed...

1 TIMOTHY 6:14–15 (THE MESSAGE)

ORDER FORM

REF	TITLE	PRICE	QTY	TOTAL
442 7	*The Road to Emmaus*	£7.99		

POSTAGE AND PACKING CHARGES

Order value	UK	Europe	Surface	Air Mail
£7.00 & under	£1.25	£3.00	£3.50	£5.50
£7.01–£30.00	£2.25	£5.50	£6.50	£10.00
Over £30.00	free	prices on request		

Postage and packing:	
Donation:	
Total enclosed:	

Name ______________________ Account Number ______________

Address ____

____ Postcode __________

Telephone Number ________________ Email ______________________

Payment by: ❑ Cheque ❑ Mastercard ❑ Visa ❑ Postal Order ❑ Switch

Card no. ☐☐☐☐ ☐☐☐☐ ☐☐☐☐ ☐☐☐☐

Expires ☐☐ ☐☐ Issue no. of Switch card ☐☐☐

Signature ______________________________ Date __________

All orders must be accompanied by the appropriate payment.

Please send your completed order form to:
BRF, First Floor, Elsfield Hall, 15–17 Elsfield Way, Oxford OX2 8FG
Tel. 01865 319700 / Fax. 01865 319701 Email: enquiries@brf.org.uk

❑ Please send me further information about BRF publications.

Available from your local Christian bookshop. **BRF is a Registered Charity**

You may be interested to know that Stephen Rand is a regular contributor to *New Daylight*, BRF's popular series of Bible reading notes, ideal for those looking for a fresh, devotional approach to reading and understanding the Bible. Each issue covers four months of daily Bible reading and reflection, with each day offering a Bible passage (text included), helpful comment and a prayer or thought for the day ahead.

Edited by Naomi Starkey, *New Daylight* is written by a gifted team of contributors including Adrian Plass, David Winter, Gordon Giles, Rachel Boulding, Peter Graves, Helen Julian CSF, Margaret Silf, Anne Roberts, Tony Horsfall and Veronica Zundel.